The Transformation
of Communist Systems

Social Change in Global Perspective

Mark Selden, *Series Editor*

Exploring the relationship between social change and social structures, this series considers the theory, praxis, promise, and pitfalls of movements in global
and comparative perspective. The historical and contemporary social movements considered here challenge patterns of hierarchy and inequality of race,
gender, nationality, ethnicity, class, and culture. The series will emphasize text-
books and broadly interpretive synthetic works.

FORTHCOMING

Women's Movements in Global Perspective, AMRITA BASU

African Women: A Modern History, CATHERINE COQUERY-VIDROVITCH

Japanese Labor and Labor Movements, KUMAZAWA MAKOTO

Power Restructuring in China and Russia, MARK LUPHER

The Transformation of Communist Systems

Economic Reform
Since the 1950s

Bernard Chavance
University of Paris VII

Translated by Charles Hauss

WESTVIEW PRESS
Boulder • San Francisco • Oxford

Social Change in Global Perspective

English edition copyright © 1994 by Editions Nathan, Paris. This translation has been revised and updated from the French original. Published with the financial assistance of the French Ministry of Culture and Communication.

English edition published in 1994 in the United States of America by **Westview Press, Inc.,** 5500 Central Avenue, Boulder, Colorado 80301-2877, and in the United Kingdom by Westview Press, 36 Lonsdale Road, Summertown, Oxford OX2 7EW

French edition copyright © 1992 by Editions Nathan, Paris
Published in French in 1992 by Editions Nathan, Paris, as *Les Réformes Economiques à l'Est de 1950 à 1990* by Bernard Chavance

Library of Congress Cataloging-in-Publication Data
A CIP catalog record for this book is available from the Library of Congress. ISBN 0-8133-1916-1 (hc.)   ISBN 0-8133-1917-X (pb.)

Printed and bound in the United States of America

∞   The paper used in this publication meets the requirements
of the American National Standard for Permanence of Paper
for Printed Library Materials Z39.48-1984.

10   9   8   7   6   5   4   3   2   1

Contents

Part Two: Systemic Adjustments

Part Three: Radical Reform

Tables and Figures

Tables

Figures

Introduction

The great transformation taking place in the former socialist countries of Eastern Europe and what used to be the Soviet Union appears as a shift from a centrally planned economy to a market economy. It consequently means a qualitative change in the economic system, which has to occur after the overthrow of old political regimes based on the power of Communist parties. For forty years (sixty in the case of the Soviet Union), these states depicted socialism as a superior alternative to capitalism. The upheaval we are witnessing is thus an event of revolutionary and historical significance. The notorious battle between systems, which went through various phases of cold war and peaceful competition, is over. Capitalism has clearly won, with the disappearance—through conversion—of its adversary.

It is vital that we understand why these last few years mark such an important turning point and that we anticipate the future evolution of these systems, because the "end of history"[1] certainly has not occurred. To do so, we have to look back at the many economic reforms that were tried in those socialist countries. In exploring those experiences, we will also see the major issues that analysts of comparative economic systems have tried to clarify: the coordination mechanisms, the role of institutions and economic agents in global regulation, and the weight of social and political forces on economic evolution.

Most important, the socialist countries' historic duel with capitalism and the way they eventually threw in the towel were both related to the attempts at reform that they pursued from the 1950s on and the complicated learning process that accompanied those attempts. That history can give us a first glimpse of many of the difficulties and dilemmas the formerly socialist countries have faced—and will continue to face—in the transition between the two systems. By putting things in comparative perspective, such an analysis can also lead us to a better understanding of the real nature and the true complexity and diversity of capitalist market economies.

---

1. Francis Fukuyama, "The End of History," *National Interest,* no. 16 (Summer 1989).

Three Waves of Reform

All economic reforms reflect the political and economic circumstances—domestic as well as international—facing the countries that enact them. The evolution of the Soviet Union itself always had a major impact on Soviet bloc countries, sometimes facilitating reform, sometimes restricting it. For socialist countries outside of the bloc per se (as in Yugoslavia or China), internal developments played a more important role, but even such countries were deeply influenced by external events, especially those in the Soviet bloc. There were three waves of reform in the socialist countries from 1950 to the time when most of those regimes collapsed, between 1989 and 1991.

The first genuine reform of the traditional system inherited from the USSR began in Tito's Yugoslavia in 1950. It was an important part of the first great political schism in the communist world. In the other socialist countries, the first reform movements were a product of de-Stalinization and its consequences. They revolved around a critical rethinking of centralized planning in the Soviet Union, the German Democratic Republic (GDR), Hungary, and Poland. In Poland, there was a real attempt to change the system of economic management for a few years following the political conflict in 1956. But it was short-lived.

The second wave of reform, more wide-ranging than the first, occurred during the 1960s. All the socialist countries were involved, with varying intensities, except for Poland and Albania, the latter being different from the others in many respects. Even the Soviet Union began in 1965 a large-scale reorganization that had been initially prepared under Khrushchev before his ouster in 1964. Also in 1965, Yugoslavia, which had been pursuing its own path for fifteen years, dismantled the remnants of centralized planning that had survived earlier reform efforts. The decade ended, however, with a general retreat from reform in Central Europe, especially with the "normalization" that followed the Soviet invasion of Czechoslovakia, which put an end to the Prague Spring. The one exception was Hungary, which was able to implement its New Economic Mechanism in 1968 and keep most of it thereafter by acting more quietly and discreetly.

During the 1970s, there was a long dry period with respect to reform, owing, most notably, to the growing conservatism of the Brezhnev regime in Moscow. Some partial adjustments were tried here and there, but without much impact. Only Yugoslavia, which sought to overcome the negative effects of earlier reforms, introduced a new system of self-management planning, but it was soon to prove a failure even to its architects.

The third wave began early in the 1980s with the Solidarity uprising in Poland. In Hungary economists pushed for more radical reforms of the economic mechanism. Gorbachev's accession to power in 1985 initiated a reformist comeback, which intensified in the following years, bringing with it criticism of Brezhnev's legacy. Throughout the decade, China, which had followed a different path during the Maoist years, began a series of reforms in agriculture, industry, and international relations which appreciably modified its economic system and development style. Those reforms were temporarily brought to a halt with the political crackdown in 1989, but the momentum picked up again in the earlier 1990s and has accelerated since then.

The revolutions in Eastern Europe in 1989 and the evolution and ultimate collapse of the Soviet Union in 1991 ushered in a wholly new era. The self-proclaimed objective of most governments of the formerly socialist countries now became the establishment of a market economy. The goal was no longer to reform the socialist system but to replace it altogether with capitalism.

A Typology of Reforms

What do we mean by "economic reform in a socialist system"? It is a large-scale program of transformation that employs a series of institutional measures designed to produce an improvement in economic performance and functioning of the system and at the same time maintains the base formed by state ownership and the single party. Typically, it relies on enlarging horizontal relations while reducing vertical links in the economy.

We can distinguish between two types of reform. First are systemic adjustments, which relax centralized planning or affect other parts of the system, such as agriculture or foreign trade, without introducing significant institutional changes. Second are radical reforms, which significantly modify some institutions (other than the base on which the whole system rests), such as discontinuing central planning or decollectivizing agriculture. If either or both of the key elements of the institutional base are transformed, we are no longer talking about reform, but of systemic dismantling. Change takes a qualitative character; it is no longer intrasystemic—reform—but intersystemic. It amounts to a "mutation," a transformation.

The analysis of reforms presented in this book is organized according to the typology above: first, the traditional system (Part 1); then, the attempts at systemic adjustments (Part 2); radical reforms (Part 3); and, finally, the systemic dismantling (Part 4). The arrangement does lead to a certain chronological awkwardness, which should in turn help illustrate

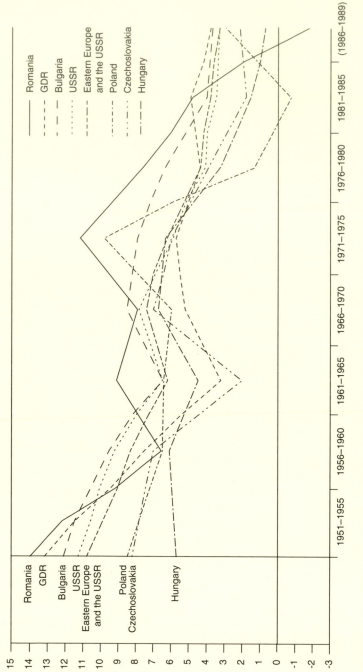

Figure I.1 The evolution of growth in Eastern Europe and the USSR according to official statistics (average annual growth rate of net material product, in percentage terms, for five-year periods, 1951–1989). *Source:* Economic Commission for Europe (UN), *Economic Survey of Europe in ...* (New York: United Nations, various years).

the point that the socialist countries took somewhat different paths. Nonetheless, this approach best illustrates the evolution of thought of the economists and reformist policymakers, an evolution that, notwithstanding the censorship and even the self-censorship practiced in these countries, constitutes an important part of this long history.

The history of reform presented here focuses on changes in the economic systems and institutions as well as the development of reformist ideas. The reader should thus place it in the larger political, economic, and social context of each period and each country. Even though they share important features with Eastern Europe's recent evolution, the complexities of Gorbachev's Soviet Union and Yeltsin's Russia are not dealt with in this book.

Part One

The Traditional System

During the ten years after World War II, the new communist regimes took different paths and moved at different rhythms in implementing radical institutional changes. Nonetheless, they all adopted a system based on what they considered to be the unquestioned model for a socialist economy—the Soviet system, which had developed in the 1930s and which seemed to have been legitimized by the victory over Nazi Germany. Soviet economic organization under Stalin was thought of as the only approach for a country trying to go beyond or bypass altogether the capitalist stage of social development. Collectivized agriculture, state-owned industry and banking, central planning aimed at producing rapid structural changes and accelerated growth—those were the goals. It was this traditional system, *copied from the Soviet Union, that the reforms since the 1950s sought to modify. The system was an organic and complex whole, with inner conflicts as well as overall consistency, which the systemic approach tries to explain.*

The history of economic reform reveals the great inertia of the traditional system, once it got established. A tendency to reproduce and sustain itself is the key characteristic of the systemic core: state ownership plus single-party control and centralized planning. Experience has shown that the classical structures of collectivized agriculture, monopoly on foreign trade, a limited private sector, and the power of directors within enterprises could be made more flexible and adaptable. These structures can thus be seen as other components of the traditional system.

The development mode associated with Stalin-era organization was determined by a number of interrelated factors. Among the most important was a strategy designed to produce rapid growth through a high investment rate and industrialization concentrated in heavy industry. The adaptive behavior of individuals and corporate groups that were placed in this world of taut planning and frequent shortages, combined with the development strategy itself, produced certain phenomena. The main characteristics of the developmental style that accompanied the traditional system were extensive growth, ever-increasing asymmetry

The Systemic Core

1. Institutional base   • State ownership
                               • Single party
2. Central Planning   • Control hierarchy
                               • Breakdown of targets
                               • Administrative allocation of inputs
                               • Administrative price setting
                               • Redistribution of profits
                               • Macroeconomic control of wage funds
                               • Monobank

Other Elements

• Collectivized agriculture
• Monopoly of foreign trade
• Restrictions on the private sector
• One-man management in the enterprise

Figure 1.1 The traditional system

in favor of the production goods sector, residual growth of consumption, lagging agriculture, autarkic tendencies, and regulation through shortages. The rigidities built into these arrangements gradually became the focus of the reformists' analysis and attention as they came to qualify and criticize Stalinist economic theory in order to create and legitimize new models for the socialist economy.

The Institutional Base

The originality of the socialist economies as a historical system lies in the combination of two seemingly heterogeneous principles: state ownership and a single-party system. Although socialist systems, like Western ones, are characterized by a commodity and monetary economy on the one hand, and by a wage labor system on the other, the former have shown a high specificity in this regard, as well as in the interplay of economic and political factors. The combination of state ownership and rule by a single party can be seen as the foundation, or institutional base, of the socialist systems, not centralized planning, which cannot exist without this institutional base.

Nationalization and State Control

Outside of agriculture, the change from private to state ownership occurred rapidly everywhere (only in China, where it took place in the mid-1950s, was compensation paid to the former owners). The state ended up owning almost all property, not only in industry, but also in the banking, construction, transportation, and commercial sectors. Although cooperatives did remain in some limited sectors, they were de facto state controlled because they were integrated into state hierarchical structures, subject to central planning, and controlled by the Party apparatus, especially through the appointment of their directors.

The Single Party

Despite the different ways communists came to power in the bloc countries, the Stalinist political model was adopted in all of them. Once in place, a single party dominated. Nonsocialist parties were normally eliminated, and sometimes the social democrats "fused" with the communists. In a few cases, microparties "allied" with the Communist Party continued to exist but had no real influence. The Communist Party's monopoly on power should be understood as that of the *apparatus*, not of all its members. The "leading role of the Party," as specified in the socialist countries' constitutions, was especially important in economic matters. Based on state ownership and the hierarchical organization of

9

State Control of Housing in Eastern Europe in the Early 1950s

Against a background of a generally low level of new construction, agencies of central or local government took over control of most of the housing stock in large and medium towns, with or without formal expropriation. The allocation of housing was already strictly in the hands of housing offices by 1950; rents were kept at a very low, sometimes purely nominal, level (save in the GDR). New dwellings in the towns were almost totally limited to the state sector and were distributed virtually free of charge, according to political and occupational criteria; the share of private construction was determined mainly by conditions in the countryside, which were unfavourable both because of the general economic situation and because of an acute shortage of building materials.

Source: Wlodzimierz Brus, *Institutional Change Within a Planned Economy,* in M. Kaser, ed., *The Economic History of Eastern Europe,* vol. 3 (Oxford: Clarendon House, 1986), p. 36.

Table 1.1 Socialized Share of Industrial Output and Total Retail Turnover: 1952

	Industry	Trade
Albania (1950)	98	88
Bulgaria	100	98
Czechoslovakia	98	97
East Germany	77	54
Hungary	97	82
Poland	99	93
Romania	97	76

Note: In 1948, Yugoslavia had reached a level roughly equal to that of Bulgaria in 1952.

Source: Wlodzimierz Brus, *Institutional Change Within a Planned Economy,* in M. Kaser, ed., *The Economic History of Eastern Europe,* vol. 3 (Oxford: Clarendon House, 1986), p. 8.

economic administration, the Party's leading role was expressed in the *nomenklatura* system, allowing it to control hiring and firing for all positions of responsibility at the various economic levels. The Party structure paralleled that of the state administration. Every level of the economic hierarchy was under the *dual control* of the Party organization at the same level and of the administrative level above it (itself controlled by the Party according to a similar setup, all the way to the top levels of the state, which were subject to the authority of the Politburo and of the Central Committee Secretariat). The dual aspect—political and administrative—of centralized economic decision making was obviously an essential ingredient in directive planning, since administrative orders could combine with mobilization campaigns and "political" control. However, the multiplication of lines of authority proved also to be a source of conflicts of interests and responsibilities.

The subordination of trade unions to the Party apparatus profoundly altered their nature. They became "transmission belts" for centrally made decisions, organs for monitoring and mobilizing a work force that was deprived of autonomous organizations for articulating its views, negotiating on its behalf, and putting forward claims.

Some Characteristics of the *Nomenklatura* System

The Party's *nomenklatura* applies to all positions of responsibility, whether they involve "elected" or appointed officials. This arrangement covers all parts of the apparatus: Party, state, unions, as well as all the so-called social organizations.

The practical impact of this system is considerable as far as the state organs are concerned. Neither national government ministries (in which personnel are appointed) nor the soviets in the USSR and the city governments in the other countries (composed of elected officials) should be thought of as institutions independent of the Party hierarchy. Appointed or elected, state officials have to go along with the Party authorities.

Moreover, the Party *nomenklatura* makes no distinction between Party members and "non-Party" officials. ...

Contrary to what one might think at first, the *nomenklatura* does not constitute a bureaucratic system in the classical sense of the term. According to one Polish text, a "superior" Party organ can always intervene directly in the decision making of one "inferior" to it, that is, without following normal hierarchical procedures. Thus, one of the classic rules of the bureaucratic system has been abolished. The same holds for the rule permitting the immediate firing of administrative officials, apparently without appeal. ...

A number of functions in several sectors of the apparatus (administration, economy, security, etc.) are subject to a double *nomenklatura:* of the Party and of higher levels of the state hierarchy. The Party organs' decisions have priority over those of other organs. One can thus say that state functions are subject to a double control, unlike responsible positions in the Party itself.

Source: T. Lowit, "Y a-t-il des Etats en Europe de l'Est?" *Revue française de sociologie* 20, no. 2 (1979): 443–444.

2 Central Planning

Economic planning was formally put into place when an interconnected set of institutions and procedures, first developed in the Soviet Union, was copied by the East European countries during the late 1940s and early 1950s (mid-1950s for China). At the heart of that planning system was the state-owned industrial sector. As had been the case in the Soviet Union since the 1930s, the planning system was supposed to carry out an ambitious strategy for development and structural change. Doing that became possible because of the unified system of ownership and the high centralization of political and economic power.

The Comprehensive Control Hierarchy

All of state industry was part of a single hierarchy organized along sectoral lines, that is, according to production branch. At the top, the government and Party leadership constituted the *center*, of which the Central Planning Commission, which mirrored the Soviet Gosplan, was a part. The intermediate level consisted of the branch (or technical) *ministries*, each of which had a clearly defined part of the productive apparatus under its jurisdiction. In addition to its functional departments (general services), a ministry had, for each sub-branch, a chief administrative organization, the equivalent of the Soviet *glavki*. The chief administrations were in charge of the operational management of enterprises. They supervised all aspects of the production plan: the supply and turnover of goods (assured by the central agencies for supply and sales), the determination of prices, the wage fund, and relations with financial agencies. The number of chief administrations varied from country to country. There were also some differences in the way each ministry's jurisdiction was divided. Sometimes, their number was quite large, as in Poland, where the Ministry of Heavy Industry had twenty chief administrations in 1951. Finally, the *enterprise* made up the third level, at the bottom of the hierarchy in the state sector. The position of the enterprise is perhaps best reflected by the status of its director, whose appointment, evaluation, and career as a whole were determined by the ministry.

The Ministerial System

Detailed planning and direct supervision of the day-to-day activities of lower economic entities required of an economic ministry a substantially narrower scope, compared with its position as a sectoral centre of economic policy-making; hence the proliferation of economic ministries created by the division of those previously existing. In none of the people's democracies was their number lower than ten at the peak of the Stalinist period, save in Albania where there were six; Poland had at the same stage twenty-six economic ministries (including three in construction alone, and another three in transport). This in turn required some coordination even within the government—hence the high number of vice-premiers overseeing a cluster of cognate ministries: ten in Czechoslovakia, nine in Poland, six in Bulgaria and Romania, five in Hungary and Albania; the GDR had five vice-premiers in 1950 and seven in 1954 with the distinction, however, that the majority of them belonged to the other parties subordinate to the communists.

Source: Wlodzimierz Brus, *Institutional Change Within a Planned Economy,* in M. Kaser, ed., *The Economic History of Eastern Europe,* vol. 3 (Oxford: Clarendon House, 1986), p. 14.

Industrial Ministries	Urban Construction
	Industrial Construction
	Energy
	Metallurgy
	Chemical Industry
	Mechanical Industry
	Light Industry
	Agricultural Industry and Food Production
	Small Industry and Handicrafts
Agricultural Ministries	Agriculture
	Forests
	State Farms
Transportation Ministries	Railroads
	Road Transportation and Aviation
	Navigation
Trade Ministries	Domestic Trade
	International Trade
General Economic Ministries	Finances
	Public Control
	Local Economy

Figure 2.1 Economic ministries in Poland during the middle 1950s. *Source:* Jan Marczewski, *Planification et croissance économique des démocraties populaires,* vol. 2 (Paris: Presses Universitaires de France, 1956), p. 316.

An important side effect of the combination of state ownership with hierarchical organization along branch lines was that the creation of new enterprises was the exclusive responsibility of the sectoral or central administration. Because ministerial specialization was in theory extremely strict, neither the lowest (enterprise) nor the intermediary levels of the hierarchy (not to mention private actors) could transfer capital from one production branch to another. That could only be done by those at the top of the economic apparatus through the centralized process of accumulation described below.

Breaking Down the Goals

The imperative version of central planning was introduced in the Soviet Union under Stalin. The planners first developed quantitative macroeconomic goals for the economy as a whole and then broke them down and divided them up among the branches (ministries). The latter eventually broke them down among their enterprises. This process of disaggregation of the central plan's quantified figures into intermediate level, production sector goals, and then into mandatory targets at the microeconomic level for each enterprise was at the heart of the way the traditional socialist system worked. The hierarchical organization of the state sector allowed the formulation of detailed demands for the individual enterprise, whose annual operating plan amounted, in theory, to nothing more than a portion of the ministry's plan, and the latter was, itself, only a portion of the national plan. In such a system, officials at the various levels of the hierarchy were evaluated by their superiors on the basis of the degree to which they met the plan's goals assigned to them.

The Administrative Allocation of Inputs

In addition to the vertical demands regarding planned production, the horizontal relationships that the enterprise had to maintain with its suppliers and customers were also regulated. The enterprise's customers were designated from above (retail outlets for consumer goods, other enterprises or supply agencies working as "wholesalers" for intermediary goods). Similarly, supplies used for planned production were provided by separate enterprises or by a ministerial supply agency according to an administrative order resulting from the plan. The supply of needed intermediary goods was thus the product of a form of *rationing*, because it required the director to get a certificate from the ministry for all planned deliveries. Even though market forms for the sale and purchase of goods remained, money and prices played a relatively passive role, and one of the vital aspects of competition—the ability of an enterprise to change suppliers or find new customers—had been eliminated. The centralized supply system was frequently disrupted, in consequence, compromising planned production. Directors tried to protect themselves in different ways, such as overstocking and hoarding inventory or establishing informal horizontal relationships with other enterprises, to obtain needed material.

The Bureaucratic Setting of Prices

Once the traditional system was in place, the leadership also adopted a method of setting prices that mirrored the Soviet model of the 1930s. That system had three main characteristics. First, economic decision makers at higher levels, not the enterprise, determined prices and, in so doing, the enterprise profits, since both prices of intermediary goods needed for production and wage levels were regulated as well. Second, once inflation had been brought under control during the first half of the 1950s, in China and Eastern Europe there was a policy of stable prices, which often remained unchanged for years. Finally, retail prices were generally determined according to a principle of balancing supply and demand, whereas wholesale prices were calculated according to an

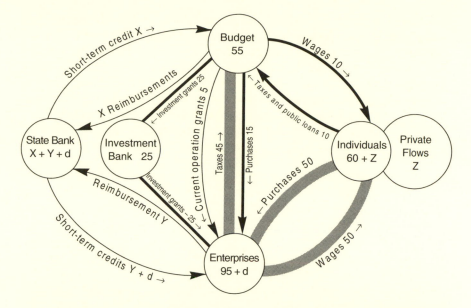

Figure 2.2 The flow of money and finance in the people's democracies: a simplified view. These figures represent the approximate percentages of national income. The relative importance of short-term credit from the State Bank cannot be determined, since statistics on the circulation of money have been published only in East Germany. Short-term credits supplied to the state ("X") are assumed to be equal to reimbursements since, as a general rule, budgets are balanced. However, the credits "Y + d" granted enterprises are greater than reimbursements by an unknown amount "d," since in an expanding economy, working capital must be increasing. This increasing "d" contributes to the financing of production and is thus incorporated in the national income of the following period. To the official and strictly regulated exchanges should be added a private one, also of unknown magnitude "Z," which represents the transactions between the consumers, private artisans, and private farmers. The depreciation circuit has been excluded to keep the chart from becoming too complex. *Source:* Jan Marczewski, *Planification et croissance économique des démocraties populaires*, vol. 2 (Paris: Presses Universitaires de France, 1956), p. 411.

average planned cost to which was added profit at a rate determined at the branch level ("cost-plus" formula). Prices of consumer goods were thus disconnected from those of production goods in what amounted to a *heterogeneous* price system.

Budgetary Redistribution

In setting prices this way, the administration determined, on the one hand, the enterprise and the branch's profits and, on the other, the difference between wholesale and retail prices, which varied from product to product. The latter amount represented the *turnover tax,* a "tax according to difference," levied mainly on consumer goods, with the

The Discretionary Nature of Profits Centralization
at the Enterprise Level in the Soviet Union

The manner in which the withdrawal of profits was organized until 1965 demonstrates that despite appearances, there was confusion between the finances of the state and those of the enterprises, a confusion that ran absolutely counter to the principle of financial autonomy. In effect, the withdrawal of profits amounted to a "redistribution tax": it was planned for the budgetary year at a global level, calculated on the basis of estimated profits, less the minimal portion (on average, 4–5 percent) of what was left to the enterprises, and, similarly, less the amount of money to be given to the reserve funds of the economic administration. This overall sum could be increased during the course of the year if the planned level of profits was exceeded. The burden of taxation was thus distributed arbitrarily among the enterprises by the economic administration. One can easily see that in this situation the enterprise had no incentive to increase its profit. If it made more than the plan called for, the additional profits were taken away. If, in contrast, the enterprise lost money, it could always count on a subsidy to cover the deficit. To be sure, before 1965, the system allowed for the creation of "enterprise funds" for the profits, but the preconditions for creating these funds were so numerous that an enterprise could rarely meet them. Few enterprises ever tried, given the limited amount of money an enterprise could hope to retain.

Source: M. Lavigne, *Les économies socialistes soviétique et européennes* (Paris: Armand Colin, 1979), p. 335.

money going to the state's budget. Most of an enterprise's profits, too, were returned to the state. As a result, the budgetary resources of the state were drawn above all from the turnover tax and centralized profits on the basis of the Soviet formula of "two forms of mobilization of the net revenue created in the economy." The flip side of this centralization of social profit was the distribution of investment funds through budgetary allocations, determined independently of the branch or the enterprise's profitability.

Through this substantial redistribution of economic surplus, or socialization of profits and losses (themselves influenced by the setting of prices), the state balanced or modified inequalities in profitability it had directly created itself. More precisely, it disconnected real profits (or losses) in one branch from decisions about investment that the branch could take. Enterprises could not engage in self-financing or borrow money for investment on their own. The center thus had an extremely powerful tool for shaping the overall accumulation rate and for assuring that its sectoral priorities were met—two fundamental developmental goals during the Stalinist era in the socialist countries.

Control over the Wage Fund

Along with the central setting of prices for both inputs and products went a strict regulation of the wage fund allocated to each enterprise. Wage scales were also set centrally, as was the number of people employed in a given enterprise. In the traditional system, the most important planned indicators (such as the gross value of production) had an effect on the wage fund at the enterprise level. If the plan's goals were reached, the money available for wages would also be equal to that planned. If the goals were exceeded, additional funds would be added. Bonuses for blue-collar workers, unlike those for managers, were not an important factor, however, before the reforms of the 1960s.

Regulation of wage funds and wage scales was an important instrument of macroeconomic control of the overall growth of wages and of income differentials. Thus, the conditions for the creation of value added in enterprises and the method for dividing it between wages and profits were determined by external administrative decisions (setting prices of inputs and production, control of wage fund). The main management criterion was reaching quantitative goals of production; and because of the way resources were redistributed, as already indicated, determining investment in the enterprise or branch was independent of its profitability or productive efficiency.

Active and Passive Money

[It seems that] in the centralized model, money plays an active role in the labor and consumer goods markets, in the sense that the economic figures expressed in monetary units (wages, prices) have an impact on the choices made by decision makers (workers, consumers) and that, as a result, the top levels of the hierarchy structure the work force and consumption according to their preferences. They cannot be treated simply as accounting figures in conventional terms. ...

The role of money differs as far as relations between the center and the enterprises or among the enterprises themselves are concerned. ...

The economic decisions made by the center and subordinate levels are detailed instructions for all the important forms of economic activity at the enterprise level, including the volume and the structure of production, manufacturing methods, sources of supply, and delivery channels. In these areas, money does not play an active role, influencing the real factors of the reproduction process. On the contrary, it is but a passive reflection of these factors. The enterprise makes its calculations not before but after having made (or rather, more exactly, after having received) the decisions. Money is little more than an accounting device for expenses considered indispensable to the production process determined in advance. The planned financial result (profit or loss) is but a passive reflection of the structure of indicators and mandatory prices. The possibility of changing production methods or modifying the technical coefficients through the influence of the pricing structure does not exist, since the decisions about the use of a given piece of equipment or primary good were made from above. As a result, favorable financial outcomes have no more influence in determining that an enterprise should expand than unfavorable results, that it should contract.

Source: Wlodzimierz Brus, *Problèmes généraux du fonctionnement de l'économie socialiste* (Paris: Maspéro, 1968), pp. 98 and 100.

The Monobank

The banking system inherited from the Stalinist era was a unified, or homogeneous, organization in which no distinction was made between central and other banks. The currency issued by the bank was used to pay wages and for the purchase of consumer goods by individuals, whereas all other transactions were carried out through transfers between bank accounts, which enterprises could have only at the local branches of the bank. The essential function of the banking system was thus to regulate the flow of money through these two separate circuits—cash and noncash—according to goals predetermined in the plan. The bank thus played a major role in controlling the way the plan was carried out regarding both interindustrial exchanges and the wage funds. As we have already seen, investment funds were given out by a specialized bank through a system of budgetary grants that were non-reimbursable (and did not even require interest payments). What credit the state bank did grant was used only for short-term purposes to cover the costs of current production.

At the macroeconomic level, the planners sought to balance global purchasing power (less anticipated savings, which individuals deposited in savings banks associated with the monobank) with the value of the planned supply of consumer goods plus services. In this goal, the global wage fund as well as nonwage incomes were planned for each year.

3

Other Parts
of the System

This chapter covers four other critical components of the traditional model. Though every bit as important to the system as a whole, they turned out to be more amenable to reform than the rigidly defined institutional base and centralized planning discussed earlier, as the example of agriculture shows.

Collectivized Agriculture

Although collectivization was less brutal in Eastern Europe and especially China than in the Soviet Union, the institutional framework that emerged during the 1950s was similar to that of the *kolkhoz* system. In the collective, or "cooperative," farms, land was collectively owned and cultivated except for small and restricted *family plots*. Only the state-owned Machine Tractor Stations (MTS) were allowed to buy heavy agricultural equipment. The MTS would then rent the equipment to the collective farms, giving the MTS considerable leverage over what the kolkhoz did. Stalin developed a *tributary* policy for agriculture. Farms had to sell their produce to the state at fixed prices, which were always set very low. In Eastern Europe (though less in China), the terms of trade between agriculture and industry deteriorated sharply during the 1950s. A small number of state farms that were managed like industrial firms coexisted with the cooperative farms, which were dominant, once collectivization was completed.

The Monopoly on Foreign Trade

In the area of international economic relations, state centralization created an air lock between national producers and their foreign partners. Prices for goods imported and exported by national enterprises were set by the planning agency. Sales and purchases were conducted by the central trade organizations. Goods were bought from and sold to foreign countries at international market prices, and the profits and losses stemming from the difference between those prices and the ones deter-

Stalin and the Machine Tractor Stations

In 1952, Stalin came out against a proposed reform that would have dissolved the Machine Tractor Stations (state enterprises) and sold their machinery to the kolkhoz. For Stalin, this would have reinforced an inferior form of socialist ownership (the kolkhoz one) to the detriment of a superior one (state ownership, or "of the people as a whole"). It would also extend rather than restrict the commodity sphere of the economy.

What would be the effect of such a measure?

The outcome would be, first, that the collective farms would become the owners of the basic instruments of production; that is, their status would be an exceptional one, such as is not shared by any other enterprise in our country, for, as we know, even the nationalized industries do not own their instruments of production. How, by what considerations of progress and advancement, could this exceptional status of the collective farms be justified? Can it be said that such a status would facilitate the elevation of collective-farm property to the level of public property, that it would expedite the transition of our society from socialism to communism? Would it not be truer to say that such a status could only dig a deeper gulf between collective-farm property and public property, and would not bring us any nearer to communism, but, on the contrary, remove us farther from it?

The outcome would be, secondly, an extension of the sphere of operation of commodity circulation, because a gigantic quantity of instruments of agricultural production would come within its orbit. What do Comrades Sanina and Venzher think—is the extension of the sphere of commodity circulation calculated to promote our advance toward communism? Would it not be true to say that our advance toward communism would only be retarded by it?

Source: Joseph Stalin, *Economic Problems of Socialism in the U.S.S.R.* (New York: International Publishers, 1952), pp. 68–69.

Table 3.1 Socialization of Agricultural Area in Eastern Europe (1952–1957)

	1952		1953		1954		1955		1956		1957	
	(1)	(2)	(1)	(2)	(1)	(2)	(1)	(2)	(1)	(2)	(1)	(2)
Albania	–	6	–	8	8	9	–	15	31	34	58	61
Bulgaria	53	61	60	63	–	–	61	64	63	–	87	90
Czechoslovakia	34	43	33	43	29	42	29	43	33	49	51	68
GDR	3	–	12	30	14	28	20	33	23	30	25	34
Hungary	25	37	26	39	18	31	22	34	9	–	12	–
Poland	5	17	7	19	8	19	11	24	9	22	1	13
Romania	5[a]	–	11[a]	25	11[a]	24	13[a]	26	13	38	20[a]	48
Yugoslavia	13[b]	–	3[b]	–	2[b]	23	2[b]	–	–	23[b]	–	–

(1) Percentage in collective farms.
(2) Percentage in collective and state farms.
[a]Including tillage associations.
[b]Peasants' working cooperatives only.
Note: Data usually relate to the last quarter of the year; in some instances the sources differ substantially because of variant definitions of land (agricultural or arable), of cooperative (with or without looser associations), or of cooperative holdings (including or excluding private plots). Thus the comparability of the figures as far as absolute levels are concerned is poor, but they reflect the general direction of changes.
Source: Wlodzimierz Brus, *Institutional Change Within a Planned Economy,* in M. Kaser, ed., *The Economic History of Eastern Europe,* vol. 3 (Oxford: Clarendon House, 1986), p. 52.

Table 3.2 From Private Farming to Collectivized Agriculture in China: 1950–1958 (% of peasant households)

	1950	1951	1952	1953	1954	1955		1956					1958			
						June	Dec.	Jan.	Feb.	June	Dec.	Apr.	Aug.	Sep.	Dec.	
Mutual aid teams	11	18	40	39	58	50		n.a.	n.a.	n.a.	n.a.	n.a.				
Elementary APCs	–	–	0.1	0.1	11	14	59	50	36	29	9	–	–	–	–	
Advanced APCs	–	–	–	–	–	0.03	4	11	51	63	88	100	70	n.a.	n.a.	
Rural people's communes	–	–	–	–	–	–	–	–	–	–	–	30	98	99		

Note: APCs = Agricultural production cooperatives.
Source: Carl Riskin, *China's Political Economy* (New York: Oxford University Press, 1987), p. 86. Reprinted by permission of Oxford University Press.

mined by the planners domestically became part of the state budget, not that of the enterprises involved. Exchange rates played a totally passive role. This system was called *Preisausgleich,* or price equalization. Enterprises had no direct contact with their foreign partners, and domestic prices were disconnected from world ones, in much the same way that domestic wholesale prices were divorced from retail ones. This pattern was to be found in relationships with other socialist economies (the Council for Mutual Economic Assistance, COMECON, founded in 1949, included during the 1950s Albania, Bulgaria, Czechoslovakia, Hungary,

The Shift in the Structure of Foreign Trade

[In addition to the geographic reorientation of trade], the adoption of the Soviet development strategy by the people's democracies can be seen in the structure of the products they imported and exported. Trade among the socialist countries was characterized from the outset by a preponderance of machinery and other equipment. In 1953, such goods already made up a third of all trade, a figure that grew during the years that followed. The two most industrialized countries— Czechoslovakia and the GDR—were "assigned" the role of supplying equipment to the less advanced countries, including the Soviet Union. By 1953, two-thirds of East German exports consisted of machinery and equipment, above and beyond the material seized as postwar reparations payments. The Czechoslovak economy, for its part, went through a true conversion. It exported fewer and fewer manufactured consumer goods (the share of textiles and glass products dropped from 31.6% in 1937 to 9.9% in 1953) and sold more and more machinery (9% in 1937, 40% in 1953). Similarly, these goods reached 45% of all Bulgarian imports in 1951, a proportion comparable to that in the Soviet Union during the First Five Year Plan (FFYP). The same trend can be seen in the countries at an intermediate level of industrialization, but they were also in the process of becoming exporters of equipment, with Hungary the most extreme example.

Source: Jean-Charles Asselain, *Plan et profit en économie socialiste* (Paris: Presses de la Fondation Nationale des Sciences Politiques, 1981), p. 98.

the GDR, Poland, Romania, and the Soviet Union), as with the Western ones. The national currencies were nonconvertible.

The fundamental goal of this monopoly on foreign trade was to give the state control over all foreign exchange—both its volume and its structure—and integrate it into the system of central planning and to protect the economy from the dangers of unmanaged openness. One sometimes spoke, then, of the socialist economies' *trade aversion,* at least with capitalist countries. During the 1950s, all the new socialist countries, including China but not Yugoslavia, reoriented their trade toward the "socialist camp."

Marginalizing the Private Sector

During the Stalinist years, the Soviet Union virtually eliminated the private sector, except for the small private plots on collective farms. Although the other socialist countries never went quite that far, they all implemented restrictive policies, which the figures reached in the 1960s illustrate. The only partial exceptions were the GDR, where a significant portion of the retail and industrial sectors remained in private hands, and Yugoslavia and Poland, where much of agriculture was reprivatized.

Stalin had introduced private plots initially in 1935 as a concession to the peasants who had been forced to collectivize. Over the years, the plots became political ping pong balls, as policy periodically shifted between increased central control and liberalization in each of the countries, with the authorities, nevertheless, looking on them as an annoying vestige of private ownership. Elsewhere, the number and size of legal private enterprises were strictly limited. They were limited, too, to what were considered to be minor economic sectors, such as handicrafts, restaurants, retail sales, and the like.

One-Man Management of Enterprises

The Soviet principle of *yedinonachaliye,* that is, the undivided authority of the enterprise director, should be included among the important components of the traditional system. Although the directors were entirely under the authority of the ministry that appointed, evaluated, and fired them, they were the absolute rulers within their own enterprise. The Party committee certainly wielded some power, but the directors themselves were members of the committees. The key point is that the workers were excluded from all participation in management, a powerlessness that was reinforced by the fact that the trade unions were under

Table 3.3   The Socialized Sector in 1967 (%)

	Agricultural Land	Industrial Output	Retail Sales	National Income
Bulgaria	99	99	100	95
Czechoslovakia	90	100	100	95
GDR	95	88	79	94
Hungary	94	99	99	96
Poland	15	100	99	76
Romania	91	100	100	95
USSR	98	100	100	96
Yugoslavia	16	98	n.a.	77
Weighted average	92	99	98	95

Source: J. Wilczynski, *Socialist Economic Development and Reforms* (London: Macmillan, 1972), p. 3.

the control of the Party and the director. Hopes for self-management that existed in certain countries, such as Czechoslovakia during the late 1940s, were stifled, but their reemergence during the political crises of later years played an important role in the history of reform, which we will consider next.

4 The Socialist Economy in Stalinist Doctrine

The doctrinal justification for the traditional system was not developed in a systematic fashion until rather late. Drawing support from the Stalinist theses of the Soviet Constitution of 1936 and from Stalin's work on historical materialism in 1938, the classical formulation of "the political economy of socialism" was found in The Economic Problems of Socialism in the USSR, *which Stalin published in 1952, just a few months before his death, and in the* Textbook of Political Economy *of the Soviet Academy of Sciences (1954). Both texts were translated in all the "brother" countries and had a deep and lasting impact on the way economic theory was developed and taught.*

Stalinist political economy was to play an important role in two contradictory ways. On the one hand, it inspired conservatives, who strove to maintain the traditional system for the next thirty years. On the other, it was the beginning of the evolution of reformist economic thought, which can be interpreted as a gradual but growing intellectual emancipation from the Stalinist dogmas.

The "Contrasting" Model

In Stalinist thought, the "socialist mode of production" was seen as the mirror image of capitalism. Socialism was to follow capitalism in the process of historical evolution because socialism overcame the contradictions that would lead the capitalist system to its collapse: class and other social conflict, competition, anarchy, recessions and depressions, and even war. In the socialist system, the economy and society were in essence united, homogenized, and organized under the principle of state ownership and the single party. Its supporters were convinced that socialism's superiority over its rival would be particularly easy to see in its higher rate of economic growth, which would occur because the economy had been freed from the shackles imposed by capitalism's relations of production (the private-ownership system). Stalin's slogan formulated in 1928, "To catch up with and overtake the advanced capitalist countries," was adopted by the other socialist countries during the

Capitalist Hell and Socialist Paradise

The contrasting models of a declining capitalism and a victorious socialism had its first theoretical presentation in a book by Soviet economist Eugen Varga published in 1937 and distributed worldwide in translation (the English title is *Two Systems: Socialist Economy and Capitalist Economy*). The table of contents provides a good idea of what his argument was like:

1. Capitalist accumulation and socialist accumulation.
2. The development of material forces of production under capitalism and in the Soviet Union.
3. Industrial production under capitalism and in the Soviet Union.
4. Non-utilization of fixed capital under capitalism. Complete utilization of productive plants in the Soviet Union.
5. Output of labor under capitalism and in the Soviet Union.
6. Chronic mass unemployment under capitalism. Full utilization of the labor force in the Soviet Union.
7. The intensification of the market problem under capitalism and its disappearance in the Soviet Union.
8. Agrarian crisis under capitalism. Growth of agriculture progress in the Soviet Union.
9. Depreciation of currency under capitalism. Strengthening of Soviet currency.
10. Tendencies of capitalist economy to decline. Systematic construction of socialist economy.
11. The regulation of economy under capitalism. Planned economy under socialism.
12. The impoverishment of the proletariat under capitalism. Improvement of workers' conditions in the Soviet Union.
13. Mass ruin of peasants under capitalism. Their rise to material and cultural well-being in the Soviet Union.
14. National and colonial oppression under capitalism. Freedom and equality of all nationalities in the Soviet Union.
15. From bourgeois democracy to fascism; from tsarist absolutism to true democracy.
16. The fascists want world war. The Soviet Union defends peace.

The Great Depression in the West, combined with the absence of reliable statistics on the Soviet Union during the 1930s, made such a propagandistic depiction somewhat credible. After the war, its supporters claimed it was confirmed—in a marginally modified way—by the expansion of the "socialist camp" and its high rates of growth.

Source: Eugen Varga, *Two Systems: Socialist Economy and Capitalist Economy* (New York: International Publishers, 1939).

1950s. Their leaders were convinced that this was not simply a slogan, but a real possibility, given socialism's *systemic advantages*.

Socialist Ownership

What defined the system was the structure of ownership. Socialist or social (that is, owned by society) ownership took two forms, which were all but sanctified by the propagandists. State ownership was the *superior form* because the property supposedly belonged to "all the people"; it dominated the economy. Kolkhozian (or collective) ownership was that of specific groups of people. Its degree of socialization was, in other words, limited, and collective property was thus considered an *inferior form*. Private ownership was not included as a category in the socialist economy at all, because it was seen as a leftover, a transitory type destined to disappear under the higher phase represented by communism. The transition to this final stage of development would also bring the transformation of collective into "all people's" (that is, state) ownership. For these reasons, Stalin opposed selling the Machine Tractor Stations to the kolkhoz, and Mao lauded the creation of people's communes bringing together a number of agricultural cooperatives as a step toward communism.

Socialist Commodity Production

Why did the socialist economy have commodities and money itself, which Marxist tradition had long considered to be components of capitalism? According to Stalin, the reason was the existence of the two forms of socialist ownership. In exchanges between state industry and collective farms, there was a modification of owner, which produced a genuine commodity relationship. Consumer goods were true commodities. That was not the case, however, for means of production, produced and exchanged within the state-owned sector. Here, as with wages, commodity categories (money, prices) were simply accounting and management instruments used to facilitate the overall, coordinated planning of the economy. Commodity (noncapitalist) production and the "law of value" thus did exist in the socialist economy, but in a limited context and in a planned framework in which their operation was transformed as they became planning instruments. When the transition to communism occurred, the unification of the ownership systems would render all these features obsolete, and the economy would thus rid itself of all commodity and monetary components, in conformity with the traditional dogma.

The Socialist Mode of Production

Socialism is a regime based on social ownership of the means of production under two forms: state property (of the people as a whole), and cooperative property (including collective farms). It is a regime in which the exploitation of man by man has disappeared, in which the national economy develops according to a plan in order to satisfy the ever-increasing needs of the workers while always increasing production on the basis of technical superiority, and in which is applied the principle of distribution according to work.

Source: Académie des sciences de l'U.R.S.S., *Manuel d'économie politique,* 2d ed. (Paris: Editions sociales, 1956), p. 400.

Commodity, the Law of Value, and Money

1. The existence under socialism of two principal forms of socialist production, state production and collective production, make[s] commodity production necessary as well. Commodity production and circulation are above all limited to goods for personal use. Under socialism, commodity production is commodity production of a particular nature, without private ownership of the means of production and without capitalists. It is for the service of the socialist society.

2. In a socialist economy, the commodity has a use value created by the concrete labor that went into making it and a value created by abstract labor. Socialist society ignores the contradiction between private and social labor. In a socialist economy, that use value and the improvement of the quality of production are extremely important. ...

3. The law of value has, in a socialist system, a limited field of action. It does not regulate production but influences it and has a regulatory impact on market circulation. The planned management of the national economy makes use of the law of value. Its action is taken into account in prices planning.

4. In a socialist society, money is a general equivalent. It is an economic instrument for planning the national economy at the same time that it is used to keep track of and control the production and distribution of the social product, to measure the labor expended and to measure consumption.

Source: Académie des sciences de l'U.R.S.S., *Manuel d'économie politique,* 2d ed. (Paris: Editions sociales, 1956), p. 497.

Planning

In Stalinist doctrine, the idea of a *planned economy* had a dual and ambiguous meaning. It implied that the system was subject to state planning but also that it was developing in accordance with the plan, at least potentially. Planning could lead to an organized economy, in sharp contrast with capitalist competition, which is synonymous with anarchy. That possibility existed because of the organizational and social homogenization (the unity of interests) that socialist ownership provided, owing to the hierarchical unity in the economy as a whole, which in some ways made it look like a single giant enterprise. The division of labor became technical rather than social, and the regulation of microeconomic activity was linked with a mastery of macroeconomic proportions and of the major directions of overall development.

Possibility and Reality: Planning Errors

The apologetic and rather crude statements of the 1930s did not admit that any dysfunctional or disproportionate outcomes were possible in a socialist economy. In 1952, Stalin sought to modify that position somewhat. Using the "contrasting" method, he claimed that there was an "objective law" built into the system:

> Our yearly and five year plans must not be confused with the objective economic law of balanced, proportional development of the national economy. The law of balanced development of the national economy arose in contradistinction to the law of competition and the anarchy of production under capitalism. It arose from the socialization of the means of production, after the law of competition and anarchy of production had lost its validity. It became operative because a socialist economy of a country can be conducted only on the basis of the economic law of balanced development of the national economy. That means that the law of balanced development of the national economy makes it *possible* for our planning bodies to plan social production correctly. But *possibility* must not be confused with *actuality*. They are two different things. In order to turn this possibility into actuality, it is necessary to study this economic law, to master it, to learn to apply it with full understanding, and to compile such plans as fully reflect the requirements of this law. It cannot be said that our yearly and five year plans fully reflect the requirements of this economic law.

Stalin did not suspect that this new dogma and his theses on socialist commodity production and the law of value were to open the door to a (timid) reformist orientation.

Source: Joseph Stalin, *Economic Problems of Socialism in the U.S.S.R.* (New York: International Publishers, 1952), pp. 11–12.

Part Two

Systemic Adjustments

The initial reforms can be thought of as systemic adjustments, or attempts to perfect the traditional system. The reformers hoped to make the system more rational and flexible without modifying its basic principles. The goal of these reforms was to better harmonize the behavior of individual workers, enterprises, and the state. They were thus concentrated on improving management methods within the framework of central planning, in particular, offering incentives and other stimuli, especially for enterprise directors.

At one point or another in their histories, virtually all the socialist governments tried these types of systemic adjustments. We will consider three typical examples: Poland, whose theoretical influence on later development was considerable, the Soviet Union, which mattered because of its ideological and political "leading role," and East Germany, which exhibited a certain originality in this area.

Poland: Pioneer and Then Laggard (1956–1979)

October 1956 and the First Wave of Reform

In 1956, the Polish political landscape was rocked by a revolt against Stalinism and the desire for "socialist renewal." That year saw the beginning of radical change in the aftermath of the Twentieth Congress of the Communist Party of the Soviet Union (CPSU), held in February. The year was marked by the workers' revolt in Poznan, the October uprising, and Wladyslaw Gomulka's return to power. The first workers' councils appeared, and the decollectivization of agriculture began. The reformist experiments begun in 1956 were not themselves to last long, but they would remain the most important ones Poland would see until 1980, and they would have an important intellectual impact on reforms in other countries.

An Economic Council, which would function alongside the government, was created. It was headed by Oskar Lange and included some of the most prominent economists in Warsaw (Czeslaw Bobrowski, Wlodzimierz Brus, Michal Kalecki, and Edward Lipinski). It engaged in a dialogue in which the various positions in the ensuing public debate were already present, including the two extremes. On one side were advocates of markets such as Stefan Kurowski, who condemned centralized planning as contrary to democracy and the sovereignty of the consumer. On the other were defenders of the status quo. In the academic community, however, a consensus, which was expressed in part in the *theses* published by the Economic Council in April 1957, emerged. In this view, central management should be limited to overall macroeconomic objectives, primarily through control over investment. Decisions at the enterprise level, however, should be made more autonomous, influenced by the center more through "economic instruments" than administrative commands.

Although the theses had an impact on the reformist policies actually adopted, the latter were only partially implemented and lost much of

The Polish "Theses" of April 1957

Even though they contained a number of compromises, the "theses on certain directions of change in the economic model" published by the Economic Council headed by Oskar Lange and received positively by the government in July 1957 represented the cutting edge of reformist thought in the 1950s. Its authors advocated "raising central planning to a superior level." The theses demanded that the central organs rely primarily on "economic instruments" (that is, financial incentives) in order to achieve the plan's targets while using administrative means in a secondary or subsidiary way. Mandatory targets should be eliminated (except under special circumstances) along with the rationing of inputs except for primary goods in short supply. Profitability should guide the behavior of enterprises. Administrative commands and the economic stimulants should not contradict each other. Autonomous investment by enterprises should be developed using retained profits or bank credit. They would have to pay interest on funds allocated for investment, which would still exist, although they would get access to depreciation funds. The enterprise incentive system should no longer be tied to performance in carrying out production plans. A material stimulation fund should be established to provide long-term incentives. Wages funds would remain controlled from above but could be modified by the enterprise on the basis of its net output (and not gross output as had been the case before). The two-tier price system (wholesale/retail) should be eliminated. A needed reform of producers' prices would occur, taking into consideration the realistic calculation of unit costs, world prices, and costs for the most important producer for each good, and should eliminate all enterprises with a "planned deficit." As for the setting of prices, the state should have recourse here, too, only to "indirect regulation" over production and the market. Price reform should represent the beginning of a reform period lasting two years. Finally, the theses argued that "democratizing the management of the national economy calls for the active participation of employees, workers' councils, local authorities, and Parliament in the development of the plans."

The Polish authorities published the theses of the Economic Council and much of the discussion about them in several languages. They received widespread distribution among economists in the neighboring socialist countries.

Source: Excerpted from and based on Wlodzimierz Brus, *Institutional Change Within a Planned Economy,* in M. Kaser, ed., *The Economic History of Eastern Europe,* vol. 3 (Oxford: Clarendon House, 1986), pp. 97–99, and Michael Montias, *Central Planning in Poland* (New Haven: Yale University Press, 1962), pp. 277–278.

their coherence, especially after they began to lose the support of the political leadership. They did reduce the number of obligatory indicators for enterprises and the number of products subject to centralized allocation. Enterprise funds permitting the payment of bonuses linked to performance were established, and a law on workers' councils was passed. These councils were to be freely elected and operate independently in the production units. In theory, they also had the right to oversee the management and even the appointment of the director.

However, Gomulka and his colleagues at the top of the party apparatus were not in favor of radical measures, and once the fever of 1956 had subsided, the momentum for change was curbed. The renewed influence of the centralizers reached a peak with the neutralization of the workers' councils and their transformation into Conferences of Workers' Self-Management in 1958. A third of the delegates were still elected by the workers, but the rest were appointed by management, the union, and the Party committee.

Wlodzimierz Brus's Decentralized Model

In *The Market in a Socialist Economy,* written in 1959–1960 and published first in Polish in Warsaw in 1961, Wlodzimierz Brus presented the key themes of this first wave of reform (and the second as well) with remarkable theoretical clarity. Even though he accepted the Stalinist definition of a socialist economy (state ownership, the end of exploitation, and distribution of income according to work done), he distinguished between the general principles underlying a socialist regime and the different "functioning models," which represented various forms of the latter. Thus, the centralized model in effect until then should not be equated with socialism as such because socialism could also exist in a "decentralized model." This argument was typical of the "revisionist" Marxism of the period, which sought to present Stalinism as a version of socialism, valid only for its time or distorted from the beginning. It legitimized political and economic reform as consistent with the true principles of socialism, which were still believed to be superior to capitalism. According to Brus, the question of whether it was necessary to use the market mechanism should be treated, not from an ideological viewpoint, but in a more practical way: Could it help as an "instrument" in socialist planning? Brus answered his own question in the affirmative and proposed a package of reforms that did not affect the institutional base but did propose eliminating the breaking down of plan targets and central allocation. The central authorities would use indirect economic levers while keeping a decisive influence over investment and price setting.

Brus's Model

In the functioning model of socialist economy, defined as planning with a regulated market mechanism, Wlodzimierz Brus built his analysis around two central actors: the state and the enterprise.

The center develops a macroeconomic plan based on long-term "social preferences." This plan deals with growth in production, the division of national income between accumulation and consumption, main sectoral and regional investment targets, modifications of the income structure, employment and labor productivity, and the volume and composition of foreign trade. But the plan's indicators would not be mandatory. They would not be broken down to the enterprise level, which would make its own ongoing decisions independently without the central allocation of inputs and outputs. Having profitability as its only goal—a synthetic success indicator—the enterprise would only be expected to meet general guidelines imposed by the center, which would influence it mostly through "indirect measures" regarding prices, wages, taxes, credit, customs duties, and foreign currencies. "The active role of money, not only in the consumer goods and labor markets but within state property itself, is used to reach the same types of goals as those achieved in an authoritarian way through physical planning under the centralized model." The author emphasized the compatibility between such a system of decentralized planning and workers' self-management, which "finds an economic base for its practical achievement in a system of management that gives the enterprise a certain freedom in its decision making."

Source: Wlodzimierz Brus, *Problèmes généraux du fonctionnement de l'économie socialiste* (Paris: Maspéro, 1968), pp. 175–182 and 195.

The 1960s

Although it had been the reformist pioneer during the 1950s, Poland found itself lagging behind during the 1960s when the second wave of reform spread in neighboring countries. A timid attempt to get reform going again was made from 1965 until 1968 with some partial modifications based on local experiments, but for the most part these had little practical impact. Despite the "antirevisionist" purge, in which the reformist economists were among the principal victims, following on the heels of the 1968 political crisis, the theme of economic reform surged into the limelight again toward the end of the decade, especially around the questions of incentives and the price system (a first restructuring of wholesale prices had been implemented in 1960). Slated to go into effect on January 1, 1971, the reform called for a new way of calculating the administered price of production goods; it introduced price ceilings in certain cases and allowed prices in some other cases to be determined contractually. At the retail level, significant price increases were expected for food as part of a general austerity program aimed at containing inflationary pressures that had built up in recent years (freezing of wages funds until 1972 at their 1970 level was planned). Announced crudely just before Christmas in 1970, these increases led to the workers' revolt in Gdansk. The protest movement was quickly suppressed, but it did contribute to Gomulka's fall. His successor, Edward Gierek, began his rule by canceling the price increases and the new system for economic stimulation. This first "veto" of the Polish workers represented a critical step on the path that led the country to Solidarity and led Eastern Europe as a whole to the events of 1989.

Gierek's Strategy and the "Large Organizations"

During the 1970s, Gierek adopted a voluntarist strategy calling for accelerated growth, attempting to combine an improved standard of living with a strong expansion of investment. It was an extreme case of a search for "import-led growth," especially in technological areas. This policy, which envisioned a growing export capacity enabling deferred payment, led to growing disequilibriums, most notably in the size of the international debt, and eventually to the explosion of 1980. At the same time, however, periodic pressures for systemic adjustments continued.

In 1973, an industrial concentration policy was adopted around the "large economic organizations" (WOG), which sought to combine the advantages of more-simplified management for the ministries and increased autonomy for the larger, consolidated economic units. In 1976, there were 110 of these WOG, which were responsible for two-thirds of all

Relaxation in Foreign Trade

Several other measures prepared under Gomulka for introduction at the beginning of 1971 were retained by the leadership. These concerned the reform of producer-good prices and particularly the reorganization of the foreign-trade system where two important moves were envisaged. The first was a break in the monopoly of the foreign trade organizations (*centrale handlu zagranicznego*) subordinated to the Ministry of Foreign Trade, for industrial ministries and associations could now obtain permission to organize their own foreign-trade enterprises or to arrange their export business through a specialized foreign-trade corporation on a commission basis; this led to a substantial increase in the direct involvement of industry in foreign trade, especially where manufacturing for export was concerned. Secondly, as in Hungary and the GDR, the *Preisausgleich* was in principle to be replaced by charging users of import[s] or seller[s] of exports the so-called "transaction price," which was the foreign currency price converted into zloty by a coefficient for the respective currency area (for Western convertible currencies, for the clearing of accounts—mainly with developing countries—and for the transferable ruble zone of COMECON). Actual practice never fully corresponded with this simple rule, but the change affected the financial interest of industrial enterprises and hence their behavior with regard to foreign trade.

Source: Wlodzimierz Brus, *Institutional Change Within a Planned Economy,* in M. Kaser, ed., *The Economic History of Eastern Europe,* vol. 3 (Oxford: Clarendon House, 1986), pp. 197–198.

sales in industry and services and 61 percent of total employment. In particular, WOG classified as "pilot units" gained a large degree of autonomy in determining employment and wage levels as a function of how much "added production" (that is, roughly, value added) they had achieved. This field, which became sensitive because of wage increases that many deemed excessive, is one of the areas in which economic recentralization from 1975 on could most easily be seen. The powers given to those pilot units regarding the retention of profits, access to credit, and decentralized investment exacerbated the problem of excess accumulation that grew out of the center's overall development strategy. The swing of the pendulum toward centralization during the second half of the 1970s, however, did not add to the government's ability to exert macroeconomic control because in multiplying its corrective priorities, it lost control over the way the system evolved.

In early 1980, a more radical and wide-ranging reform than that of 1973–1975 was envisaged at the same moment that the increased economic tensions reached a boiling point: declining production, shortages (and rationing), inflation, growing foreign debt, and balance-of-trade problems. The revolution of August and September 1980, which led to another change in the political leadership, the legalization of strikes, the recognition of Solidarity as an independent trade union, the granting of some civil liberties, and a wage increase of 10 percent, was the result of the combination of the workers' and opposition movements' development and the economic crisis. In December 1981, the country plunged into a bizarre period that combined the state of emergency and a permanent social crisis with attempts at radical economic reform.

Relaxing Central Controls on Wages and Employment

The employment and wages policy, which had previously been determined by higher authorities, was now given to the WOG and their components according to the following rule: The growth rate of the wage fund was to be a proportion (R) of value added (R varied in different branches and enterprises from 0.3 to 0.95, i.e., it was always lower than 1.0).

This provision amounted to a built-in mechanism for the reduction of the share of wages in value added, and can be interpreted as the micro-economic counterpart of a macro-economic policy of rising accumulation and other non-consumption expenditure (as a share of national income), as well as a provision for a contingency reserve, or safety factor. Excess wage (and workers' bonus) payments over the disposable wage fund could be financed by borrowing (at a penal rate, and with managers forfeiting their own bonuses), while any surplus over actual payments could be carried over as reserves. In theory, this formula introduces the possibility of raising average wages by reducing the growth of value added and employment, but there is no evidence that corporations followed restrictive employment policies—on the contrary, their new powers led to a continued pressure on the labour market.

Source: Domenico Mario Nuti, "Industrial Enterprises in Poland: 1973–1980," in Ian Jeffries, ed., *The Industrial Enterprise in Eastern Europe* (New York: Praeger, 1981), p. 43.

6

Big Brother Modernizes:
The Soviet Union
(1957–1985)

Throughout the period between the Twentieth Congress of the CPSU and Mikhail Gorbachev's accession to power, Soviet authorities made a number of attempts at systemic adjustment (1957, 1965, 1973, 1979, and 1983). The attempts varied in scopes but all had disappointing results.

The *Sovnarkhoz*

Nikita Khrushchev's sudden reorganization of economic administration carried out in 1957 targeted "departmentalism" in the branch ministries while seeking the support of local Party officials and organizations. Sectoral ministries were replaced as the bodies controlling enterprises by Regional Economic Councils (*sovnarkhozy*), which directed all enterprises located in their area whatever their branch. This reorganization sought to reconcile central management with the diverse regional conditions of such a massive country—a goal that China also would pursue on several occasions. This change in the control hierarchy quickly led to such problems as localism and regional autarky, which in some respects were analogous to those found in the traditional "departmentalism" along sectoral lines. The return to the principle of direction by branch was gradual in the early 1960s and definitive with the reform of 1965.

Khrushchev introduced another institutional change in agriculture in 1958. Stalin's doctrinal opposition was forgotten, and the Machine Tractor Stations were eliminated. Their equipment was sold to the kolkhozy, which were now authorized to own and buy agricultural machinery.

The 1965 Reform

In 1965, Prime Minister Aleksey Kosygin introduced a reform that would lead to significant systemic adjustments. It had been prepared during debates that took place during the Khrushchev years. Into the political economy of socialism inherited from Stalin's time changes were gradu-

A First Critical Examination of the Incentive System

In 1955, a professor from Kharkov who would become well known later proposed replacing gross production with profit as the success indicator for determining bonuses (profitability, established according to central norms varying from branch to branch, was then defined as a ratio of profit to net cost). He emphasized several defects in the methods being used at the time:

> In the current systems of paying bonuses, it seems that material self-interest comes into play only after the execution of the plan, whereas it plays no role before and, at times, even seems to run counter to it. It is known that the plan's targets are determined for enterprises essentially on the basis of past results. That is why an enterprise that performs poorly is sometimes given relatively modest targets, and the burden of fulfilling the plan is imposed on enterprises that do well. Thus we often see a tendency on the part of an enterprise to conceal its potential to avoid being assigned targets that are too high.
>
> Often, the plan addressed to enterprises is the outcome of a "competition" of a particular type between ministerial directors and enterprises. Practical experience shows clearly that such a process leaves great room for randomness and arbitrariness in designating quotas for the enterprises and that it by no means guarantees the full utilization of productive reserves. It is the enterprise, more than any other organization, that understands its real resources for growth in and improvement of production and that can mobilize them fastest and most effectively if it has a greater material interest in doing so.
>
> Since the entire incentive system is based on exceeding the plan, innovation makes it harder and not easier for an enterprise to receive a level of reward that matches its efforts. This is precisely why workers so often, openly or not, delay the adoption of scientific methods, avoid really trying promising experimental techniques under the pretext of "struggling for the plan," and are inclined to keep making old models, using decrepit technology. It unfortunately follows that the method that serves to encourage the execution of the plan frequently gets transformed into a method for encouraging technical stagnation.

Source: E. Liberman, "Calcul économique et intéressement matériel des travailleurs dans l'industrie," *Voprosy Ekonomiki* (Economic Questions), no. 6 (1956), published in French in "La réforme économique en U.R.S.S.: La discussion 1955–1965," *Notes et Etudes Documentaires* (Documentation Française), no. 3564 (Feb. 17, 1969): 11.

ally introduced, the result of contentious discussions over economic calculation, the choice of investments, or the proper formula for determining prices. The majority of economists had acknowledged that "commodity and money relations" were actually present in the entire economy, including the state sector; their explanations, however, remained divergent and inconsistent. The Mathematical School (L. Kantorovich, V. Nemchinov, V. Novozhilov) began research projects on "optimal planning" and reintroduced into economic theory some "marginalist concepts," which had been banned until then (utility, scarcity, calculations at the margin). Following the well-known 1962 article by Yevgeni Liberman in *Pravda,* a debate began in the press about incentives and profit as (planned) criteria for measuring enterprise efficiency.

Kosygin's reform proposals had several facets. An administrative reorganization reestablished sectoral ministries while reinforcing functional administrative authorities (such as *Gosnab,* which was responsible for central supply). The planning system reduced the number of mandatory indicators (to nine) for each enterprise and put the emphasis on production *sold* and on profitability. An improvement in the incentive system was sought so that enterprises could retain a portion of their profits to finance funds under their control (for bonuses, social services, and autonomous investment). Finally, the system of administered wholesale prices was modified in 1967 to reduce the variation in profitability among the branches; the two-tiered price system was maintained, however, since retail prices were not affected.

Failure and Periodic Reorganization

The 1965 reforms were in some respects contradictory because they centralized some areas of economic life while decentralizing others. In the end, they failed for a number of political and economic reasons. The shift toward profit as an incentive was at odds with the administrative determination of prices and the continued disaggregation of planned targets. Autonomous investment could not be expanded because the centralized supply system and other centralized features were kept. Conservatives blamed the rapid rise in wages after 1965 on the new incentive system. Most important of all, Brezhnev's conservative instincts rather than Kosygin's modernizing wishes carried the day more and more after the suppression of the Prague Spring in 1968. Only the centralizing aspects of the reform survived into the 1970s.

Kosygin's 1965 program also concentrated enterprises into associations in order to increase specialization, take advantage of the econo-

Nemchinov's Proposal

One of the great figures in the Soviet Mathematical School was V. Nemchinov, who died in 1964. During the debates that preceded the 1965 reform, he had put forth a critique of the system as a whole and sketched out an alternative model. He had a serious impact on reformers in other countries as well, including, for example, Czechoslovakia.

According to Nemchinov, the country had to find an "optimal combination of centralization with the democratization of economic management," which he called "a cost accounting planning system." Very few mandatory indicators would remain in the central plan, which would act mostly by setting long-term norms that would be legally binding on all economic actors, such as ratios for deductions from profits for incentive funds and branch norms for investment effectiveness. The banking and financial systems would play a major role in transmitting information and macroeconomic management. Enterprises would be free to conduct their economic activity, such as marketing and acquisition of capital goods (a wholesale trade replacing the central allocation of inputs). They would control their own depreciation funds. Profitability would determine what the enterprise does. In such a system, freely established, legally binding *contracts* would be drawn up between enterprises but would still have to be limited by "norms" determined by the center. The state would place orders, after which signed contracts would become binding on everyone concerned.

Source: Moshe Lewin, *Political Undercurrents in Soviet Economic Debates* (Princeton: Princeton University Press, 1974), pp. 177–179.

In introducing the idea of reciprocal rights and obligations between lower and higher levels of the hierarchy (an idea picked up again by Kosygin in 1965), Nemchinov emphasized the incoherence of the planning process:

> The organs situated on top do not bear any responsibility to the enterprises, as a general rule, for the errors in proportions during the elaboration of the plan. The plans for production, the labor force, finance, credit, material and technical supply, are often not consistent with one another. The reason for this is that the various parts of the economy are subject to separate planning processes. The current planning mechanism is seen in a way that each line and each column of the plan do not rest on a common organizational base. Changes introduced for some indicators of the plan do not lead to changes in the others. Reciprocal obligations do not always come in the form of contracts between those who give the orders and those who fill them. Contractual discipline remains extremely weak.

Source: V. Nemchinov, "Le système d'exploitation socialiste et la planification de la production," *Kommunist,* no. 5 (1964), published in French in "La réforme économique en U.R.S.S.: La discussion 1955–1965," *Notes et etudes documentaires* (Documentation Française), no. 3564 (Feb. 17, 1969): 37–38.

Systemic Adjustment as a Factor in Modernization

In his report on the 1965 reforms, Alexei Kosygin pointed to a number of problems in the economy. Growth rates were declining in national income, industrial production per unit of fixed capital, and labor productivity. Agriculture and sector B (consumer goods industry) were lagging. In addition, there were difficulties in material supplies. Funds for major infrastructural projects were too widely "scattered," pushing completion further and further into the future. Enterprises were too slow in adopting new inventions and technologies in production.

> The Presidium and the Council of Ministers of the Soviet Union have attentively analyzed the shortcomings that exist in the national economy and have uncovered the cause of the slowdown in the rate of economic growth. Analysis shows that the well-known difficulties that exist in the development of our economy are of a temporary nature and should be quickly overcome.
>
> According to the Presidium and the Council of Ministers of the Soviet Union, we must direct attention to the perfection of methods and forms of management for industry, when dealing with problems resulting from the further development of industry and of the elevation of people's standard of living. The forms of management, planning, and stimulation currently in effect in industry no longer correspond to the technical and economic conditions of the level of development of the forces of production.

It made sense to link incentives for the workers with the improvement of results at the enterprise level, to gain a greater flexiblity in planning, to be able to adapt rapidly to short-term changes and to the evolution of popular demand, and to accelerate technical progress.

> All this can be obtained only once central planning is allied with the economic initiative of the enterprises and collectivities, with the reinforcement of economic levers and material incentives for productive development, and with a global "accounting" economy. Then the system of economic management will have sufficiently adapted to lead to a rise in productive efficiency. The propositions made before the assembly are inspired by the essential role of centralized planning in the development of our economy. To turn away from that principle would lead inevitably to the loss of the advantages of a planned socialist economy.

Source: Alexei Kosygin's Report on Economic Reform to the Central Committee Plenum, September 27, 1965. Translated from the French version in *Notes et études documentaires* (Documentation Française), no. 3241 (Nov. 30, 1965): 5–7.

mies of scale, and reduce administrative costs. This move toward socialist "oligopolization" can be seen in the majority of the systemic adjustments (VVB [see Chapter 7] and later combines in East Germany, WOG in Poland). In 1973, the Soviet Union began a new version of the concentration policy by creating "production" or "scientific and production associations" (the latter connecting enterprises to research institutes) and "industrial associations," which were ministerial administrations (*glavki*) that were to transform themselves into superenterprises that would have accounting autonomy (*khozraschet*). But although industrial gigantism did increase following the adoption of these measures, the desired fusion came slowly and incompletely. These groups often existed only on paper. Classical behavior patterns persisted, while the power of the ministries was reinforced.

A new 1979 decree illustrated Leonid Brezhnev's style of periodic reorganizations in which some occasional hints at broader systemic adjustments were found, but the critical issue of the interdependence of the problems considered before was moved off center stage. The decree emphasized principles that were rarely respected in practice: The plan was supposed to be feasible, balanced, and stable. It was not to be modified downward to the level achieved after implementation. The notion of contracts was reaffirmed. The principle of giving the five-year plan priority over the annual one was proclaimed. A mandatory indicator measuring value added (normed net product) was to play a key role in an attempt to eliminate any incentive to use overly expensive inputs. The underlying logic was to impose new indicators that would limit the negative effects of those already in existence, namely, volume of production taking quality into account; total value of sales; increases in labor productivity; maximum number of workers employed; total profit (instead of profitability); cost reductions; introduction of new production techniques; and so on.

This last reorganization, in fact, amounted to a recentralization and did not prevent the increasing stagnation any more than did the short-lived experiments attempted later under Yuri Andropov and Konstantin Chernenko. The Soviet Union would have to wait for Gorbachev for a renewal of the spirit of 1965, which would, in turn, itself gradually be radicalized.

The Large-Scale Experiment, 1982–1985

During the interregnum that separated Brezhnev from Gorbachev, there was another attempt to correct the deficiencies of centralized planning by modifying its procedures. The experiments were limited to a few enterprises or ministries and, in principle, were to be gradually extended. The essential measures were as follows:

- The reduction of the number of compulsory plan indicators.
- Planned contractual delivery obligations become of the highest importance. Thus for every 1% underfulfillment of delivery plans the material incentive fund is reduced by 3%, while if these plans are all punctually fulfilled, the fund is increased by 15%.
- Additional material stimuli are provided for technological innovation, with greater possibilities of using own resources and bank credits. ...
- Greater stress is laid on "final results," to discourage waste of intermediary products [and stimulate cost reduction]. ...
- Instead of the "traditional" wages fund, which set hard limits on the enterprise's wage payments, there are to be long-term "norms" relating wages to output, and to the normed value added. ...
- There is much emphasis on "stable norms and normatives." ...

Source: Alec Nove, *The Soviet Economic System,* 3d ed. (London: Allen and Unwin, 1986), p. 84.

7

An Original Way:
East Germany
(1963–1989)

The New Economic System

After echoing the Soviet "Liberman debate" in 1962, the following year the East German leadership launched the second wave of reform in communist countries, that of the 1960s. Two years after the Berlin Wall went up, Walter Ulbricht presented the principles of the "New Economic System," which had been developed under the direction of two Party secretaries, Erich Apel and Günter Mittag. All the typical aspects of systemic adjustments could be found in the East German reforms: optimism about the system, attempts at modernization, partial modification of the institutions and processes of centralized planning, and growing awareness of the connections between changes in the various economic arenas. In the guidelines adopted in July 1963, the former system of management was described as ill suited to the new phase of "intensive development," which the country was entering. The New Economic System was to combine centralized planning and a "broad application of material incentives in the form of a complete and coherent system of *economic levers.*" The latter would be indirect management instruments (which were to play a dominant role in the 1968 Hungarian reforms). The emphasis was placed on financial indicators—sales, costs, and profits—in evaluating enterprise performance.

The new system was implemented during the rest of the 1960s. It noticeably reduced the areas in which the means of production were rationed, loosened control over wages and employment, and restructured wholesale prices (in 1967, prices for primary goods were raised 70 percent; semifinished goods, 40 percent; and finished goods, 4 percent). It also increased the role of profit as a success indicator and as an incentive as well as for self-financing, although the center did keep control over most investment.

Two original contributions of the reform should be underscored. First, the power of the monobank was reduced in 1967 when specialized banks were created (such as the commercial and industrial bank); under the control of the central bank, they obtained a certain degree of freedom in granting investment credit and setting interest rates. Their role in evaluating projects on the basis of expected profitability was increased. Second, there was the typically East German effort toward *intermediary centralization,* best seen in the VVB (*Vereinigungen Volkseigener Betriebe*), or enterprise associations, equivalent to the Soviet *glavki.*

In the New Economic System, the status of the VVB was changed. Their new role was as a grouping of enterprises under administrative control (actually, they had a mixed economic and administrative character). As associations of enterprises, the VVB gained accounting freedom (the Soviet *khozraschet*) and were judged and rewarded on the basis of the profit they made. Integrating research and production, the VVB took over some of the prerogatives previously assigned to the branch ministries: setting of material balances, elaborating norms, regulating of wages and investment, and distributing some profit and depreciation funds among the enterprises. It amounted to an intermediate level of centralization in which both the ministries and the base-level units lost influence in an attempt to produce a cybernetic, flexible regulation of centralized management. Sections of the new specialized banks were attached to one or more VVB (of which there were about eighty). In certain ways, this model is reminiscent of the prewar German cartels or the Japanese *zaibatsu.* The VVB served as a model for other countries during this second wave of reforms and would reappear in the system of combines during the 1980s.

As far as decentralizing foreign trade is concerned, certain enterprises were granted the right to export their goods directly and retain some of the hard currency they earned, but such reforms were less innovative than the ones just delineated. In fact, they were also in the other East European reform packages of the same period in one form or another.

Recentralization During the 1970s

The relative flexibility added to the centralized model by the 1963 reform had been made possible by partially limiting the planners' ambitions and reducing the tautness of the plan. However, the imbalances resulting from the regained voluntarism seen after 1968, linked to the "structural planning" of sectoral priorities, would lead to movement in the opposite direction. That was especially true once the events in Czechoslovakia in 1968 and Poland two years later strengthened the shift away from reformism. The New Economic System was renamed the Economic System of Socialism in 1967 and was wiped out after Erich Honecker succeeded Ulbricht in 1971. Various decision-making powers

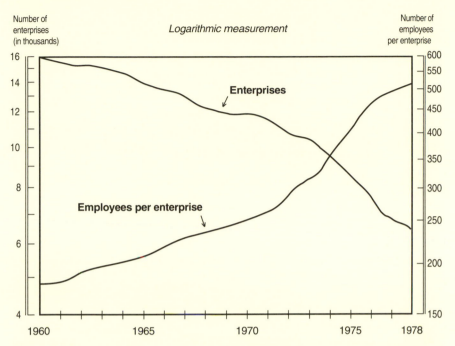

Figure 7.1 The concentration of industry in East Germany. The concentration of base-level units, the enterprises, went on throughout the 1960s and 1970s. *Source:* Manfred Melzer, "Combine Formation and the Role of the Enterprise in East German Industry," in Ian Jeffries, ed., *The Industrial Enterprise in Eastern Europe* (New York: Praeger, 1981), p. 108. An imprint of Greenwood Publishing Group, Inc., Westport, Conn. Reprinted with permission.

that had been given to the VVB were rapidly taken back by the ministries. From 1971 to 1973, many of the enterprises in the private and semi-private sectors that still existed in the GDR were nationalized. The shocks of the early 1970s—the increase in the materials imported from the Soviet Union and the Western economic crisis—also reinforced this shift back toward more central control.

Combines

In 1980, a reversal took place in "perfecting" (*Vervollkommnung*) the system when a new type of intermediary centralization was introduced, the combines, which became, in Honecker's words, the "backbone" of East German economic organization. Numbering about 150 and covering the entire industrial sector, they differed from the old VVB in that they were strictly economic, and the accent was placed as much on vertical (involving various forms of supply) as on horizontal integration. They amounted to giant monopolies, bringing together twenty to forty

Table 7.1   The Principal Combines in the GDR

Name of Combine	Number of Employees (1987–1988)
VEB Petrolchemisches Kombinat, Schwedt (petroleum products)	30,000
VEB Qualitäts-und Edelstahlkombinat, Brandenburg (high quality steel)	38,000*
VEB Kombinat Elektromaschinenbau, Dresden (electrical machinery)	30,000
VEB Werkzeugmaschinenkombinat "Fritz Heckert," Karl-Marx-Stadt (machine tools)	30,000
VEB Werkzeugmachinenkombinat "7.Oktober," Berlin (machine tools)	22,000
VEB Kombinat Polygraph "Werner Lamberz," Leipzig (printing equipment)	16,000
VEB Kombinat Textima, Karl-Marx-Stadt (textile machinery)	35,000
VEB Schwermaschinenbaukombinat TAKRAF, Leipzig (heavy construction equipment)	40,000
VEB Kombinat Mikroelektronik, Erfurt (micro-electronics)	65,000
VEB Kombinat Robotron, Dresden (calculators, computers)	68,000
VEB Carl Zeiss, Jena (optical equipment)	69,000
VEB Kombinat Haushaltsgeräte, Karl-Marx-Stadt (household appliances)	28,000*
VEB Kombinat Musikinstrumente, Markneukirchen/Klingenthal (musical instruments)	24,000*
VEB Kombinat Baumwolle, Karl-Marx-Stadt (textiles)	70,000
VEB Strumpfkombinat ESDA, Thalheim (hosiery)	16,000

* In 1986.

Source: D.I.W., *Economic Bulletin,* Apr. 1989, cited in "Panorama de l'Europe de l'Est," *Le Courrier des Pays de l'Est,* nos. 309–311 (Supplement, 1990).

enterprises and 5,000 to 70,000 employees (on average, 25,000), and through their strategic planning, the combines reduced the burden of centralized management, obtaining considerable autonomy for internal redistribution and rationalization. The enterprises that performed relatively poorly in one branch thus found themselves subject to the authority of the director general who often was, himself, the director of the combine's leading enterprise.

A number of adjustments to the traditional system occurred around the same time that the combines were created. Numerous and substantial readjustments in determining administered prices had been carried out during the second half of the 1970s, especially to take international changes into account. However, these increases were limited to wholesale prices and durable goods. Subsidies for a growing number of everyday consumer goods (food, transportation, housing, electricity) were sharply increased. Special rules introduced for new products allowed enterprises to earn larger profits for a period of two or three years. As was the case for the Soviet Union after the 1960s, the enterprises profitably used these provisions to multiply the number of "new products," many of which never existed before. In another change, in 1982 and 1983, the traditional indicator of gross production (the "production of industrial goods") became less important than four others: net profit, net production, production of consumer goods and services, and exports. The combine and enterprise directors, however, continued to receive (from above) around a hundred mandatory indicators. Finally, beginning in 1984, a "contribution to social funds" was implemented through an especially heavy tax on the wage funds (70 percent) in an attempt to force the combines and enterprises to reduce their overemployment. The measure did not have the anticipated effects.

For a period, the combines seemed to offer a tempting alternative to radical reform, an alternative that prompted the interest shown in them during the 1980s by Czechoslovakia, Bulgaria, and even the Soviet Union during the first years Gorbachev was in power. The advantages attributed to them included gains in the economy of scale (overestimated by the socialist countries for a long time), better integration of research and production and thus a more rapid diffusion of innovation, reduction in the problems of supply as a result of more internal self-reliance, easier access to foreign trade, which was somewhat decentralized, and increased bargaining power for the enterprises vis-à-vis the center in the planning process.

Despite the increased flexibility this model offered compared to the classical ministerial system, the combines quickly produced new problems of their own. The gigantism and the monopolistic nature of the combines entailed significant central control, especially regarding prices. The center worked out a relatively incoherent mix of direct and indirect (parametric) controls. The lack of competitive pressures limited the comparison of performance inside the economy. Small and medium-sized enterprises, with their capacity for innovation demonstrated by international experience, were unable to develop. The duplications and the loss of specialization because of the desire for self-sufficiency were at odds with efficiency, especially in the case of machinery and semifinished products (but also consumer goods, each combine being ordered to devote at least 5 percent of its productive capacity to them). More generally, the development of the combines did not eliminate, even if in some cases it did reduce, the classic problem of shortages, nor did it stop the growth of economic, social, ecological, and, finally, political tensions during the second half of the 1980s.

Autarky and "Flexible Administration" in the Combines

[The] idea of a closed flow of production, a leitmotif in economic literature on the combine, means that it includes all the elements of an economic circuit, from research and training all the way to sales, foreign trade, and market analysis. This view was clearly stated in the report to the Eleventh Congress of the SED in 1986: "The combine's production process is designed, in principle, to begin with the primary materials and does everything all the way to the final stages in which they are transformed into finished goods. ... We must develop the combines so that they themselves produce the raw materials that will allow them to produce high-quality final goods. It is a basic condition for improving efficiency everywhere and for being able to react rapidly to the changing nature of demand." One notes a search for the maximum autonomy, if not the autarky, of each combine as well as the flexibility of enterprises in order to direct them toward demand and to reduce delays in responding to it. ...

The combine does more than bring enterprises together; it integrates them. The director general can reallocate production among the enterprises. He concentrates scientific and technical resources as well as investment at the combine level. He alone—and no longer the ministry—is authorized to intervene with enterprise directors and give them directives. For the enterprise directors, the reform creating combines was really a centralization of power, whereas for the industrial ministries and the state, it marked a decentralization. They lost some of their prerogatives. The details of the planning process and of management passed into the hands of the directors general even though the state kept the ability to determine the overall aggregates, the management of macroeconomic equilibrium, and control over a certain number of strategically important products. The director general became the key figure in the East German economy. Through an informal but institutionalized process, the person in charge of the economy, Günter Mittag, gathered the directors general together in Leipzig each year after 1981 for a "seminar," where they were asked to commit themselves to high quantitative and qualitative economic targets, thereby going over the heads of the industrial ministers.

Source: Ivan Samson, "La R.D.A. de Honecker ou la recherche d'un socialisme prussien," *Revue d'Etudes comparatives Est-Ouest* 20 (1989): 31–32.

Part Three

Radical Reform

The underlying support for radical reforms was based on a more critical assessment of the traditional system's defects and an awareness of the failure of systemic adjustment to reduce them to any significant degree. Supporters of radical reform remained basically optimistic about an appropriately redesigned version of socialism's capacity to surpass capitalism in terms of growth, rationality, and social justice. The definition of socialism was reduced to the institutional base. Planning was kept, but its meaning was altered once it ceased to be totally or partially centralized. A central theme in radical reform was the combination of plan and market. The plan would guide growth with a long-term perspective and flexible control of investment. The market would have responsibility for regulating everyday microeconomic decisions. The transformation—no longer simply the modification—of traditional planning was thus at the heart of radical reform. The change in the systemic core was accompanied by reforms in other elements: agriculture, foreign relations, the private sector, and power within the enterprise.

Four experiments with radical reform occurred in the socialist countries. The first came in Yugoslavia during the 1950s and early 1960s, where the distance from the initial Soviet model grew wider and wider. Similar reforms were tried in the second half of the 1960s in Czechoslovakia and Hungary; they would have opposite destinies. Finally, in the 1980s, the most durable attempt at radical reform took place in China in the form of authoritarian modernization.

8

Self-Management and the Retreat from Planning in Yugoslavia (1950–1964)

The important institutional changes in the Yugoslav economy beginning in the 1950s were not defined by the country's leadership as economic reforms. When they were introduced, the changes were described as steps in the construction of a new and genuine model of socialism. The key component was self-management, which would make Yugoslavia as different from Soviet-style etatism (state-directed socialism) as from Western capitalism. The criticism of the Soviet model following the break with Stalin in 1948 appeared very radical. Moreover, it was the ongoing, cumulative nature of the systemic changes that Yugoslavia adopted that made its evolution differ from the changes in the other countries we have seen so far, which were more limited and short-lived. Nonetheless, returning to the definition given in the introduction to this book, the Yugoslav experiment before 1965 amounted to a radical economic reform, *while coming close to systemic dismantling.*

Rejecting the Traditional Model

During the first postwar years, the Yugoslav leadership was quite orthodox, especially in its adoption of the traditional Soviet economic system. The leadership quickly nationalized industry and established a single party, branch ministries, central planning and allocation, active state redistribution, and a monopoly on foreign trade, while pursuing a development strategy favoring heavy industry and neglecting agriculture. In short, Yugoslavia operated under the traditional system for a few years with the one exception of collectivized agriculture, which never covered more than a quarter of all farmland and was abandoned after two years in 1951.

The 1948 Cominform resolution that condemned Titoist heresy and the subsequent blockade of Yugoslavia by the Soviet bloc—which had been its principal trading partner—forced the leadership to come up with a systemic alternative. Called "self-managed socialism," it was, ac-

Self-Management at the Enterprise Level

[After the law of June 1950], for more than a decade, the basic organizational principles of self-management [have] remained unchanged. All workers and employees of a firm constitute the *work collective*. ... The collective elects a *workers' council* ... by secret ballot. The council has 15 to 120 members elected originally for one year and more recently for a two-year period. The council is a policy-making body and meets at intervals of one to two months. The council elects a *managing board* ... as its executive organ. The board has 3 to 11 members, three-quarters of whom must be production workers. The director is the chief executive and is an ex officio member of the managing board. ...

At first, the director was appointed by government bodies. In 1952, the power of appointment of directors was vested in the commune (local government). In 1953, public competition for the director's office was introduced, and the representatives of the commune retained a two-thirds majority in the selection committee. In 1958, the workers' councils achieved parity with communal authorities on the joint committees authorized to appoint and dismiss directors of the enterprises. The present state of affairs is that the director is appointed by the workers' council from among candidates approved by the selection committee on the basis of public competition. He is subject to reelection every four years, but may also be dismissed by the workers' council.

Source: Branko Horvat, *The Yugoslav Economic System* (New York: M. E. Sharpe, 1976), pp. 157–158.

cording to its architects, characterized not only by worker participation in enterprise management but also by the combination of the plan with the market and a tendency toward the withering away of the state. The Soviet system was denounced as a bureaucratic perversion and a form of state capitalism that behaved imperialistically toward the countries it controlled. Yugoslavia began moving in a decentralizing direction after 1950. The power of the federal government was gradually reduced, and the influence of the republics, regions, localities (*communes*), and enterprises was progressively extended.

Altering the Single-Party System

The institutional base itself also underwent significant change. In 1952, the Communist Party was renamed the League of Communists of Yugoslavia (LCY). Party cells operating inside state organs were eliminated, and the upper levels of the party hierarchy lost the power to assign mandatory tasks to lower ones. The *nomenklatura* was de facto eliminated or at minimum weakened, as self-management at the enterprise level expanded and the republics and provinces gained more autonomy. Some distinction between the Party, the state, and the economic administration was introduced. Nonetheless, the Communist apparatus retained considerable formal and informal power. At its 1958 congress, held in Ljubljana, the Party claimed it wanted to play an educational rather than a commanding role, but it never went so far, however, as to allow a multiparty system. In fact, it remained a *single* party (the same held for the trade union), but it simply was less monolithic than the ruling parties in other socialist countries because of the increasing influence of the regional and local apparatus. The political system provided a counterbalance to economic decentralization, especially in Marshal Tito's ability to hold the LCY together. Nevertheless, there was no shortage of crises: the expulsion of Milovan Djilas in 1954, the Rankovic affair in 1966, Croatian opposition in 1970–1971, and so on.

Social Ownership and Self-Management

Self-management began with a basic law in 1950 that modified the complex bundle of property rights: legal ownership, management and control, appropriation (control) of product, and disposal of assets (by sale or otherwise). The 1953 constitution called for a shift from state to "social ownership," which it declared was the only genuine form of socialist ownership. The Yugoslav ideologues drew on the Marxist distinction between state and society, a distinction that had been erased in the Stalinist economic doctrine of socialist ownership. Once the hierarchy of con-

The System of Rates (1951–1954):
An Attempt to Regulate the Division of Value Added

In the indicative planning system developed primarily by the economist Boris Kidric:

> Along with monetary policy, incomes policy was expected to become another vital "steering instrument." During the period under consideration, the ... "rate of accumulation and funds" ... ought to have provided the necessary technical solution: on the basis of the assessment of productive capacity and employment potential, and of standard wage rates, both the income and the wage bill of an enterprise were estimated; the difference between income (net of depreciation) and the wage bill was defined as "accumulation and funds" (the term "profit" or even "surplus" being carefully avoided). The rate of accumulation and funds was defined as the ratio between accumulation and funds to the wage bill. The main instrument of distributing income between the enterprise and the community was the central determination of that rate (as "normative" rates), but the others were a variety of taxes. The normative rates could not, however, be uniform throughout the economy, above all because capital having been put at the disposition of the enterprises free of charge, rates had to be sharply differentiated between sectors. But even such differentiation could not prevent very wide wage differentials because enterprises were confronted by different market conditions (or, it would be better to say, with different opportunities to influence the market). Attempts to solve the problem by supplementary taxation failed, and the degree of specification by enterprise of the rates increased. As one leading Yugoslav economist commented, this "implied direct administrative interventions which were at variance with the basic intentions of this new system," and soon led to the abolition of the method of distribution on the basis of rate of accumulation and funds.

Source: Wlodzimierz Brus, *Institutional Change Within a Planned Economy,* in M. Kaser, ed., *The Economic History of Eastern Europe,* vol. 3 (Oxford: Clarendon House, 1986), pp. 23–24.

trol (branch ministries and centralized directorates) was eliminated in 1951–1952 and the independence of the self-managed enterprise was affirmed, social ownership became clearly different from state ownership. This difference gradually grew wider, when enterprises gained more control over sharing value added between wages and profit and utilizing profit, especially after 1965. The actual nature of social ownership was the source of many debates and polemics among economists and legal scholars in Yugoslavia and elsewhere. At any rate, it was no longer state ownership because the state had lost the formal title of ownership, the power of management (managers were elected, and there was no more centralized planning), discretionary appropriation (the state kept only fiscal policy and taxation), and the right to dispose of assets, which, moreover, no longer had holders.

The Division of Value Added

In 1952, mandatory deliveries to the state were abolished in agriculture, and the majority of prices were officially freed. Beginning in 1955, a system of administrative price control was adopted: fixed prices for some goods and services (electricity, transport, sugar, cooking oil), price ceilings for some production goods (metallurgical products, coal, oil), prior declaration to the Federal Price Office of all increases, and in some cases, price freezes. Inflationary pressures developed only in the 1960s. Yugoslavia thus went from the administrative fixing of prices to price control, leaving some room for maneuver in this area. The procedures for sharing the value added in the enterprises evolved with the legislation on self-management. First the "system of rates" was introduced— between 1951 and 1954—then came the "division of profits," through which salaries were broken down into two components, a fixed "accounting salary" (or minimum wage) and a second part based on the distribution of enterprise profits after taxes (on turnover and income).

At the same time, the authorities also introduced on fixed capital an interest rate of 6 percent, defined as the price to be paid for the use of social capital. In 1957, the variable component of wages amounted to nearly 10 percent of the total wage bill. In 1958, the leadership began the "division of revenue," in which the workers' council would determine how much money went to "personnel revenues" (wages) and different enterprise funds (including those for investment), all the while claiming that such categories as wages and profits no longer had any meaning. This independence really did not go into effect until 1961, when the union and the commune lost the right to actually control the division of net income and wage differentials within the enterprise. At that point, the wage drift, which first appeared in 1958, accelerated. Some econo-

The Social Investment Funds

In 1952, the federal budget was divided in two. One part covered administrative expenses; the other consisted of intervention and investment funds, especially the Fund for Basic Capital Development, which still distributed investment funds without any repayment obligation.

In 1952, the federal government concentrated just about all investment resources in its fund. ... As early as the next year, funds for crediting investment activities were formed. Enterprises established their own investment funds, financed out of profits left to them by the plan. Both measures led to a considerable decentralization of capital formation financing. The system assumed its more permanent shape in 1954, when social investment funds (SIFs) were created at all levels—federal, state, district, and communal. From that time until the latest reforms, social investment funds granted loans to business enterprises, while capital formation in the nonbusiness sector (schools, hospitals, government offices, etc.) continued to be financed out of the government budget. In 1955, special housing funds were introduced. They were financed by compulsory contributions of firms. The creation of social investment funds—which tended to multiply as time went by—had an interesting behavioral consequence. Since all levels of the government were under constant heavy pressure to invest, and funds were separated from the budget, their resources tended to be inflated beyond anything envisaged by the social plan. In the period 1955-60, the volume of investment surpassed the target established in the social plan by 20%.

Source: Branko Horvat, *The Yugoslav Economic System* (New York: M. E. Sharpe, 1976), pp. 219–220.

mists blamed the rise in inflation after 1961 on a lax monetary policy, but the elimination of control over wage increases (by means of taxation and the role of the union), which had worked fairly well until then, was probably more important.

The Decline of Central Redistribution

The self-managed firm also gained more control over investment along with its growing influence over wage distribution. Despite expanded self-financing, the degree of profit redistribution remained high until the 1960s. Although taxes filled the social investment funds, which existed at different administrative levels and remained predominant, the federal government fund's role declined, while that of the republics and, especially, the communes grew. The communes' economic power was noticeably reinforced by the constitution of 1953, which gave them expanded rights in setting local tax rates on enterprises. Communes tended to penalize profitable enterprises with high tax rates and often used that money for local political reasons to finance other enterprises' projects that were risky or too ambitious. There were frequent references to the creation of "political enterprises" by local authorities.

The real, albeit gradual, decentralization of investment during this period occurred because of a reduction in the federal government's role. From the enterprise's point of view, however, administrative control or intervention in financing remained high. Although somewhat less centralized, state redistribution did remain significant, given the growing power of the republics and communes. The role of commercial banks and credit in financing investment grew sharply during the mid-1960s, as the liberal reforms of 1965 neared.

Foreign Trade

In 1951, the earlier system of quantitative control of foreign trade by the state monopoly was replaced by a complicated mixture of subsidies and taxes on imports and exports based on seventeen "price equalization coefficients" ranging from 0.8 to 4.0. This system, designed to produce a trade structure consistent with the investment goals of the social plan, had mediocre results. It actually maintained the isolation of the domestic economy from the world market (we should note that the blockade of the Soviet bloc countries forced Yugoslavia to redirect its trade toward the West).

A more radical reform was put into place in 1961 that eliminated the multiple exchange rates and gradually replaced with tariffs quantitative restrictions on imports (with the maintenance of some import quotas

Diversifying the Banking System

In the field of investment allocation the role of the communal banks and specialized banks was substantially enhanced by the Law on Banks of 15 March 1961. Until the beginning of 1954, the National Bank, through its branch system, had a monopoly of all commercial banking operations in Yugoslavia. The Law on Banks and Postal Savings of 28 January 1954 permitted communal authorities to establish their own banks both to engage in commercial banking operations and to control the implementation of the local budget within their respective territories. For the remainder of the decade the communal banking system grew alongside, and coexisted with, the National Bank branch system.

Specialized banks—the Yugoslav Investment Bank, the Agricultural Bank and the Foreign Trade Bank—were established in the mid-1950s to manage the federal investment funds. The National Bank also gave them funds in order to extend credits on their own behalf. As a result of the Law on Banks of 15 March 1961, the National Bank ceased to perform commercial banking functions which, henceforth, became the sole prerogative of the communal and specialized banks. This represented an important decentralization of the banking function to the territorial units although, together, the three specialized banks still controlled over 65 per cent of the assets of the commercial banking system. The investment fund system itself remained intact for a further two years until its reform in 1963.

Source: Christopher Prout, *Market Socialism in Yugoslavia* (New York: Oxford University Press, 1985), pp. 24–25.

Table 8.1 Financing Investment: Composition of Investment in Fixed Capital by Source of Finance (Excluding Private Investment) (in percent)

	1948	1951	1952	1953	1954	1955	1960	1962	1964	1966	1968	1971
Social funds and budgets	99	98	98	87	74	64	52	59	36	16	16	15
Federation	60	50	95	71	50	47	37	30	7	6	9	8
States	27	41	2	11	12	9	7	9	8	3	3	3
Communes and districts	12	7	1	5	12	8	18	20	21	7	4	4
Work organizations	1	2	2	13	26	35	37	38	32	46	37	34
Business	1	2	2	13	26	27	31	30	26	39	31	27
Nonbusiness	–	–	–	–	–	8	6	8	6	7	6	7
Banks	–	–	–	–	–	1	1	3	32	39	47	51

Source: Branko Horvat, *The Yugoslav Economic System* (New York: M. E. Sharpe, 1976), p. 222, table 28. Reprinted by permission of M. E. Sharpe, Inc., Armonk, New York 10504.

and export bonuses). This new approach was motivated by the Yugoslav desire to become a member of the General Agreement on Tariffs and Trade (GATT) and was encouraged by the Western countries and the International Monetary Fund (IMF).

Social Planning

The radical nature of the Yugoslav reforms between 1950 and 1964 was a result not only of the innovation of self-management and changes in the forms of ownership but above all else of the elimination of central planning. The core of the Stalinist model was cracked at the beginning of the 1950s with the abolition of hierarchical control, of the disaggregation of goals, and of the centralized allocation and determination of wages funds, even though it took longer for the central redistribution of profits and the monobank to give way. It was thus an essentially indicative and indirect macroeconomic planning process that went into effect, retaining one major instrument for state action: control of a large portion of investment.

In 1956, state planning became "social planning," based on broader participation and consultation. The federal authorities planned the "big proportions": the rate of accumulation, the distribution of investment through the general investment fund, and the share of collective consumption. Enterprises established their production plans independently, following the "big proportions" and market signals. In the second half of the 1950s, the development strategy was changed to give consumer goods a higher priority. The late 1950s was a period of rapid growth, but the drift toward economic crisis in the early 1960s would lead to a crisis in planning.

9

Plan and Market
in Czechoslovakia
(1966–1969)

The First Wave of Experiments

In 1958 and 1959, the Czechoslovak leadership introduced a program of systemic adjustment that was quite similar to the one implemented at the same time in Poland. Three goals stood out: giving the medium- and long-term plans a higher priority than the annual operational plan so that enterprises would not suffer from the latter's instability; introducing "counter plans" made by the enterprises so that they would propose higher goals than anticipated and stop making false claims about their capacities; and partially decentralizing investment decisions. This last point was linked to the program of industrial concentration, which brought together about 400 "economic unities of production" (VHJ)—precursors of the many types of combines and other associations typical of the second wave of systemic adjustments. The price system was restructured in 1958. This reform got bogged down very rapidly, thwarted both by a political purge in the Party and by the evolution of foreign trade (fluctuations in Soviet priorities, the break with China in 1961).

Around 1963, Czechoslovakia went through the deepest recession of the Eastern European countries, a recession that followed the "second wave of industrialization," which was linked to Khrushchev's Seventh Five Year Plan and the Chinese Great Leap Forward. Investment (centralized and decentralized), which had drifted until 1961, collapsed. National income and industrial output declined in 1963—an unprecedented event in the communist world. The crisis brought the process of recentralization to completion, but it also opened the door to the shift toward radical reform by the middle of the decade.

In 1965, the vertical and horizontal concentration of industry was increased by the reduction of the number of VHJ to 102 immense "branch unities," with an average of 30,000 employees. Some experimental modifications were introduced, such as the shift from mandatory indicators

In Favor of a Generalized Model of the Market

In a review of internal studies by the Economics Institute of the Czechoslovak Academy of Sciences published in 1968, a young economist, Vaclav Klaus, best known in 1993 as the extremely free market–oriented prime minister of the new Czech Republic, criticized the limited vision of the market that was based on an analogy with "simple commodity production." We haven't succeeded, he wrote, in resolving "the problem of the commodities market without the existence of two parallel markets, which added to the price of goods the prices of the factors of production and that of capital." It was necessary to create a "monetary market," allowing the investor to make a choice between real investment and "other nonreal activities." "As long as the investor will not make such a calculation, and as long as there is no interest rate that can regulate a rational division of financial resources between commodities and monetary markets, we will not be able to reach economic equilibrium, and the system will be continually subject to inflationary pressures." The current use of credit and interest does not mean that a monetary market exists. It could only appear "when the choice as far as the destination of financial resources becomes possible, when a portion of the financial means is transformed from money considered as current value on the commodities market into money considered as financial property, when money begins to be seen as an instrument of activity by both microeconomic and macroeconomic agents, and when money represents the factor linking the present and the future. The financial market could be created by issuing a series of state, public, bank, and enterprise bonds, which would also contribute to a rational functioning of the economic system."

As for creating a labor market, one should not think of it as the same thing as introducing unemployment but rather as "an instrument to eliminate the tranquillity and false security that exist today, the static nature of the work force, its rigidity, and its lack of movement, thus allowing the introduction of dynamism and mobility in the labor force."

This line of reasoning will reappear in the 1980s, especially in the work of the reformist Hungarian writer Marton Tardos.

Source: Economics Institute, Prague, "Inflation, Wages, and Markets," in C. Boffito and L. Foa, eds., *La crisi del modello sovietico in Cecoslovacchia* (Turin: Ed. Einaudi, 1970), pp. 127 and 135.

to the use of gross income or profit as success indicators. But most important of all, this period saw the emergence of a group of reformist economists at the Economic Institute of the Academy of Sciences; the group's leader and spokesperson was Ota Sik. More and more openly, these economists proposed a plan for a new management system that was sharply different from the official line, namely, that improvement would come through systemic adjustment.

The Market and Socialism with a Human Face

The reformist ideas that set the stage for 1968 in Czechoslovakia should be interpreted in the context of this humanist and anti-Stalinist Marxism that was developed in the 1960s. This part of the Marxist tradition had been hidden for years, and its newfound supporters sought to use it in revitalizing socialist doctrine without putting the institutional base of the system into question. This trend, which carried the Yugoslav ideas or the creative "revisionism" of the Poles further, had a stimulating impact on the Czechoslovak social sciences.

One of the important themes of this renewal was the role of "social interests," as can be seen in the work of Ota Sik and of Zdenek Mlynar. In opposing the primacy of the "general interest" and of social homogeneity in Stalinist dogma, they affirmed the diversity and the potential divergence of group and individual interests in a socialist society. They argued that a complex mechanism was needed for expressing and harmonizing these interests in satisfying the "general social interest." Rather than existing in opposition to each other, the plan and the market should be combined in pursuing that goal. Key ingredients of the Prague Spring—the search for pluralist forms compatible with the system's institutional base, the revitalization of the role of trade unions, the concept of a "structured social ownership" (that is, combining different types of public enterprises with cooperatives and private companies), the theme of political and economic democracy—grew out of this way of thinking, which appeared as a "dialectization" of the traditional model.

The 1968 experiment's most original contribution to the history of radical reform lies in the connection between democratization and economic reform. It was this link that opened the door to popular support for economic reforms, which would probably not have occurred otherwise. It also, as we know, raised tremendous fears among the ruling classes of the "fraternal" communist countries and was ultimately the reason for the Soviet military intervention that put this innovative period to an end.

The Exhaustion of Extensive Development

[Extensive expansion of production] has no sense under conditions where there is a general shortage of manpower and the over-all costs of social labour (embodied and living) begin to grow faster than the growth of social production. Under these conditions and in this way normal extensive development turns into negative development that creates insurmountable obstacles to the economic covering of the rapidly growing input requirements and, in the end, will undermine the process of growth completely.

If, therefore, conditions for extensive development that in a certain initial period were justified are now gradually disappearing, and their changed conditions are not recognized in time, then the continuing orientation of economic policy, and planning and management procedures, in the direction of extensive growth must at a certain moment fail. Together with the exhaustion of extensive sources of growth, independent of the planning directives (setting rapid rates of growth on the basis of experience in the period of a thoroughly extensive growth), the rate of growth will slow down and, at the same time, contradictions will grow to the extreme between the constantly lagging social productivity of labour and the much more rapidly growing material inputs connected with extensive development.

This is the experience that the economy of Czechoslovakia has gone through.

Source: Ota Sik, *Plan and Market Under Socialism* (Prague: Academic Publishing House, 1967), pp. 56–57.

Prices, Wages, Employment

In 1965 the reform principles prepared by the economists were formally adopted, and in 1966 the Thirteenth Congress of the Czechoslovak Communist Party opted for their "accelerated implementation." The restructuring of wholesale prices was one result. Recalculated according to the Hungarian formula of "two channels" (cost plus 6 percent of capital used plus 25 percent of the wages fund), the new prices went into effect in 1967 and turned out to be higher than planned (a 29 percent increase instead of the anticipated 19 percent). Enterprises had obviously inflated their costs vis-à-vis the administered prices. In 1966, the Czechoslovaks began following the Yugoslav practice of distinguishing among three types of prices—fixed, limited, and free—with the goods and services covered by the latter two types to be expanded over time. But the rapid increase in prices unsettled reform efforts in other areas (wages, financing of investment), and their liberalization was thus quickly brought to a halt.

The first attempt in the communist world to control the expansion of wages funds solely by fiscal measures was initiated in 1966 with the imposition of a progressive tax on raises above the planned limit. But it is significant that, given the upward thrust of wages and the increase in workers' demands, this completely indirect model of regulation did not last long.

A new system for investment, also inspired by the pre-1964 Yugoslav type, was introduced in 1967. According to the reformers, self-financing based on retained profits and bank credit would become the primary sources of investment capital (25 percent and 60 percent respectively, only 15 percent coming from the state budget). The increase in their income, a result of the price reform and the reduction of planned distribution, encouraged the enterprises' expansion drive, but nevertheless it gave rise to increased and excessive dispersion of investment, which led the authorities to return to administrative control.

From 1967–1968 on, Czechoslovakia thus encountered what proved to be a major problem for radical reform. Weakening direct control over wages and investment tended to create an inflationary drift in these two areas, which the indirect means of fiscal and monetary control (credit, interest rates) proved too weak to control. The conservative leadership and broader social groups had developed a chronic fear of inflation that prompted a recentralization of economic controls and decision making.

Indirect Planning

The most important characteristic that the Czechoslovak reform shared with the Hungarian "New Economic Mechanism" of 1968—and that

The Model Proposed by the Reformists in 1966

The development of the economic reform program began around 1964 with a group of researchers who gathered around the Economics Institute of the Czech Academy of Sciences. Ota Sik, the head of the group, defended his views before the Party leadership (he was a member of the Central Committee and its economic commission). He presented the reform program to the Thirteenth Communist Party Congress but was followed by Politburo member Oldrich Cernik, who presented the official—and different—concept of systemic adjustment.

The reform proposal of the group of economists led by Professor Sik was based on the following fifteen principles.

1. The plan as an external mechanism of the functioning of economy must be supplemented by a restoration of the market as an internal, self-regulating mechanism of the functioning of a modern socialist economy.

2. In the future, the plan should determine only the basic macro-economic development. ...

3. The enterprises must be granted a measure of autonomy which will enable them to react to the changes of production conditions and of the market; therefore, they must not be subject to limitations in the form of directive plan targets.

4. The plan directives will be replaced by economic regulation. The central planning organ shall optimize economic proportions, manage and regulate the redistribution of economic incomes, regulate credits, interest, taxes, depreciation, and so forth, through legal norms (rules of the game) which will be identical for all enterprises. ... The rules of the game must be stable and long-range. ...

5. ... The specialized ministries should be abolished because their functions (coordination of perspective plans, of investments, etc.) will be taken over by enterprise associations.

6. The relationships between the enterprises and organs of state lose their nature of subordination and superiority. They will be delineated by a law which will stipulate the rights and responsibilities of both sides. ...

7. ... The concept of the monopoly of foreign trade will be revised, and foreign business transactions will be decentralized to the enterprise associations or to the enterprises.

8. ... Membership [in associations] should not be obligatory; the enterprise should have the right to choose its partners, to enter the association, or to leave it, according to its own interests and needs.

9. There should be, in principle, three kinds of prices: fixed prices, set and controlled by the center, of basic raw materials, foods, and products; limited prices (the center will determine the top and bottom limit of their movement); and free prices, which will emerge from supply-and-demand relations or from an agreement between the supplier and the customer.

10. The criterion of enterprises' activity is not the fulfillment of plan targets but the size of their *gross income,* the use of which (after the deduction of payments due), will be determined by the enterprises themselves.

11. In order to restore competition, even with the high degree of monopolization of domestic production, the entire economy must be gradually confronted with world markets. A transition to convertible currency is a long-range assumption.

12. A prerequisite of reform is a change in the level of wholesale prices which must objectivize price relations both among the branches and within them.

13. Introduction of levies on basic funds and restoration of the active role of interest rates is to emphasize the role of capital in creating values and to make rational economic calculations possible.

14. The level of wages and salaries will depend on the gross income of the enterprise. The state guarantees only the minimum basic wages.

15. The complex criterion of the effectiveness of economic management should prevent the growth of productivity of present labor being paralyzed by a decline in the productivity of capital.

Source: Radoslav Selucky, *Economic Reforms in Eastern Europe* (New York: Praeger, 1972), pp. 86–87.

Administrative Management as an Obstacle
to the Scientific and Technical Revolution

An interdisciplinary group of the Czech Academy of Sciences directed by the philosopher Radovan Richta argued that the "technical and scientific revolution" was a general and fundamental requirement in the contemporary world. In a work that had a wide national and international audience, the group criticized the current management system as being antidynamic, lacking the capacity for feedback, and having a negative impact on the "human factor."

Everything suggests that the *principal* domestic brake on the technical and scientific revolution that several socialist societies have keenly felt is the underdevelopment of their *economic structure,* of the complex of incentives and instruments for economic management that grows out of the essence of socialism. ... It turns out that we have not yet developed the economic instruments of socialism that could realistically encourage the socialist spirit of enterpreneurship, stimulate economic initiatives at all levels, properly balance the risk presented by the introduction of innovations, and punish passivity and conservatism.

The concrete experience in Czechoslovakia proves that administrative management from the center has been intrinsically linked with the stage of industrialization in which the application of science and technology on a vast scale and the universal development of human forces is not a top priority. As a result, this form of management tries to stimulate society only toward quantitative increase of production through the global fund of social labor. It does not have the ability to impose the rational utilization of social labor and, through that, the optimization of economic outcomes or efficient development. This form of management reduces the incentives of socialism to the single criterion of maximizing production as demanded by the center. In contrast, at the enterprise and individual levels, it produces and stimulates in practice a number of nonsocial, lateral petty interests and appetites that maintain the status quo (such as repugnance toward modern technology, the elimination of useless tasks, the efficient utilization of funds), which put society under the thumb of an extensive *spontaneous* movement running counter to the scientific and technological revolution. The extensive development of industrial production that only extends the current process does not draw enough on science and research or on new forms of organization and a higher level of skill among the workers. It turns out that without the complete application of radical solutions in the form of economic reforms and new management systems based on the use of the market, we cannot open the way to qualitatively new processes in a relatively industrialized socialist country.

Source: Radovan Richta, *La civilisation au carrefour* (Paris: Editions du Seuil, 1974), pp. 96–97.

made these two experiments radical reforms—was their elimination of mandatory planning and the centralized allocation of resources. Beginning in 1967, the plan's central goals were no longer being broken down into intermediate and microeconomic ones except for limited "extraordinary mandatory goals" and mandatory import-export quotas (formally abolished in 1969). The reform envisaged the center's action only through indirect "economic regulators," fiscal for the long term, monetary (and price) for the short term. At the same time, the material and technical supply system was abandoned except for a few products. Enterprises were allowed to establish direct links with their suppliers and customers. By weakening the vertical links and extending the horizontal ones, the Czechoslovaks began to create a model combining an indicative plan with the market.

Two original aspects of the autonomy the reformers wanted to give enterprises should be stressed here. In 1968, each enterprise was allowed to open ventures outside its initial area of specialization and even to form new enterprises (a right also conferred on state organs). An enterprise could also freely join larger production groups or leave them as it saw fit. To this first attempt at capital mobility was added a plan to equalize the starting conditions for enterprises. In the past, the central administration had made capital grants on a very uneven basis, and now enterprises would gradually "buy back" their capital assets over a period of seventeen years.

The Self-Management Dimension

The reformist concept of separating ownership from the state was connected to the principle of self-management, to which Ota Sik was won over in the spring of 1968 in order to attract working-class support for economic reform. During the course of the debate on self-management, three versions of it were proposed: first, one close to the Yugoslav version; second, one giving a great deal of influence to middle management and technical experts; and third, one combining the first two. During the summer of 1968 and after the Soviet invasion of the country, a certain number of workers' councils were spontaneously organized in the enterprises. Self-management was thus seen by a segment of the workers (and even the unions) as a way to organize resistance against the occupation.

The draft law on socialist enterprises proposed in January 1969 was one of the last reformist documents issued before "normalization." It called for three types of enterprises. In the state enterprises still controlled by the ministries, the authorities would name the majority of the members of the workers' council. In nonstate enterprises, the founder,

Economic and Political Democracy

A complex program of social organization was put forth at the underground congress of the Czech Communist Party, held at Visocany after the Soviet invasion in August 1968:

> In the concept of self-administration, the independent role of trade unions was to be restored. Within the enterprises, there was to be a plurality of three forces— workers' council, management, and the trade union. The trade union would represent employee interests; the workers' council would represent the interests of the enterprise owners; and management would represent business interests.

The self-administration system would be combined with a representative system and the parliament would have to take into account the views of special (auxiliary) chambers.

> Thus, the parliament's industrial chamber would be elected in the enterprises and the workshops of industrial production, trade, transportation, and material services; the agricultural chamber would be elected in agricultural (both cooperative and state) enterprises; and finally, the chamber of social services would be elected in health, educational, cultural, and scientific institutions. These chambers would have specialized powers, for instance, the right to return legislative bills dealing with their specific affairs for a second reading, to supervise state and economic management in matters under their responsibility, and so forth. The production principles of the elections would guarantee that those members of the state organs who made decisions on management and coordination of a specific work activity would be chosen from among those who were actually engaged in that activity and that they would be responsible to them, controlled by them, and appointed or recalled by them. The element of universal democracy would thus be combined with the professional element, and the state organs (plus a representative system of the classic type) would be combined with the element of self-administration.

Source: Radoslav Selucky, *Economic Reforms in Eastern Europe* (New York: Praeger, 1972), pp. 100–101.

who might be an individual or an institution, would name a majority as well. But in the "public ownership" enterprises, which would be legally independent of the administration and were expected to make up the largest group, the majority of the enterprise council, which exercised the "entrepreneurial function," would be elected by the employees, with a minority appointed by external institutions (ministries, banks, etc.). Granted control over management, the council would recruit the director through a competitive process.

Normalization

The fate of reform remained uncertain for some time after August 1968. In certain areas, progress continued to be made, as in the case of self-management, the free association of enterprises (some did that even after December), and the reduction of the administrative machinery (in January 1969, the Ministries of Mining, Energy, Heavy Industry, Chemistry, and Consumer Goods were eliminated). A law on planning that would have called for the shift to an entirely indicative system was worked on until the summer of 1969. After the dismissal of Alexander Dubcek and his replacement by Gustav Husak in April 1969, however, the reforms were dismantled in stages and the government oversaw a gradual return to the traditional system, completed in 1971 and 1972. In the process, the reformers were denounced as "right-wing revisionists" who would have created a free market economy and thus "total anarchy."

Reform and Macroeconomic Instability

Despite all its weaknesses, the Czechoslovak system introduced in January 1967 was viable. If, in 1966, tensions in the Czechoslovak economy increased (partly due to the prereform expectations of firms, as well as in 1967 in Hungary), the restrictive policy of the government in 1967 was nearly as successful as in Hungary in 1968. Growth slowed down in both countries and domestic and external balances were consolidated. The achievements of the two reforms were also similar: supply followed demand considerably better than before. In Czechoslovakia, the unprecedented explosion of consumer demand in 1968–9 was well absorbed by the growing supply of consumer goods.

True, tensions increased during these years in the economy, but one has to keep the following in mind. The new economic system created by the reforms both in Czechoslovakia in 1967 and in Hungary in 1968 eliminated most of the traditional mandatory planning, without allowing for the operation of a competitive market. Market constraints have not become really relevant for firms. Under such conditions, the formal and informal authority of the government, the feeling of dependence on superiors, plays an important role and can have a paralysing effect in the long run but a stabilising effect in the short run. In 1967 (and in the first quarter of 1968), this factor was fully in force in Czechoslovakia, as well as in 1968 and later in Hungary. From March to April 1968 onwards, with the simultaneous growth in political power of the party leadership, the authority of the government over the economy gradually collapsed. Wage and investment demands, which the government could no longer resist, cumulated. The vulnerability of the system was seen to be particularly acute under such conditions.

Source: Tamas Bauer, "Success and Failure: Emergence of Economic Reforms in Czechoslovakia and Hungary," in K. Dopfer and K.-F. Raible, eds., *The Evolution of Economic Systems: Essays in Honour of Ota Sik* (London: Macmillan, 1990), p. 255.

10 Hungary's New Economic Mechanism (1968–1979)

The Hungarian reform of 1968 was the product of a number of economic commissions that had been working on it for several years. After 1963, their efforts were led by Reszö Nyers, Central Committee secretary responsible for economic affairs and the true architect of the New Economic Mechanism (NEM). One of the unique characteristics of this reform was that it created a certain consensus not only among economists but also between them and the political leadership, with Nyers playing an important role linking the two. The "Kadarism" of the 1960s had been a kind of enlightened state absolutism that, though sometimes indicted as "goulash communism," actually provided the setting that made broader reform possible. The reform was deliberately limited to the economy without any spillover into domestic politics or international relations. Putting the New Economic Mechanism into effect required some compromises, such as the retention of the ministerial structure and the creation of administrative regulatory "brakes." Although the NEM would not have been possible without these compromises, at the same time they were obstacles to its thorough implementation; that situation revealed a general contradiction in economic reforms.

Like the Czechoslovak reforms introduced at the same time, the NEM had its roots in the "decentralized model" developed by Wlodzimierz Brus. It was a system in which the macroeconomic plan was linked to a "regulated market" through the intermediary of regulators. The latter constituted the "economic instruments" through which the government would influence the economy, thus replacing the traditional administrative directives. The market would thus be guided in an indirect manner according to general goals through parametric, or uniform, instruments: prices, wages, taxes, credit, and so on. The goal of reform was in fact the establishment of a new type of planned economy somewhere between the traditional directive model and a French-style indicative system. Although central management and allocation of resources were abolished, the state kept responsibility for developing a general plan. What seemed to be in some respects an "economic policy in the framework of state ownership" thus went beyond day-to-day management of economic activity by the government.

The Concept of Economic Mechanism

One of the contributions of the Hungarian School was the distinction its economists drew between the formal "system of control" and the real economic relationships reproduced in the actual functioning of the system. Laszlo Antal thus defined the *economic mechanism:*

> Beyond planning, the system of incentives and financial regulators, the organizational system of the enterprises, and the organs of economic control (which make up the system of economic control), one includes the decision-making mechanisms by higher levels, the informal relations between institutions of economic control, social organs, and the enterprises as well as the real distribution of decision-making power between the different levels (which did not necessarily correspond with the legal rules in place), and the internal control and motivation of enterprises. Behind all that, we find the system of interests and power relationships. The automatic actions, behavioral norms, and the reactive and adaptive responses heavily influenced by these factors also come into play here. During a given period, the real functioning of an economic system can be characterized by all these essential and relatively stable elements.
>
> In taking all these elements into account, the system of economic control includes all the factors that can be directly influenced by the center. ... [By changing the system of control, the center could try to influence relationships based on interests and social relations. But if] this dynamic does not put itself into gear or if it leads in the direction of automatic reactions or of processes that did not coincide with its intentions, the changes initiated by the center will not have the intended effects or will seem to have them only in a formal or superficial sense. In effect, the economic mechanism is characterized primarily by the relationship between the enterprises and the different institutions, the real system of influence and decision making, notably at the top, the concrete division of labor among the enterprises, the possibilities offered to economic actors, as well as their motivations at all levels—that is, precisely those factors for which direct regulation is hardly possible.

Source: Laszlo Antal, "Développements avec quelques digressions: Le mécanisme économique hongrois dans les années 1970," in J. Kornaï and X. Richet, eds., *La voie hongroise: Analyses et expérimentations économiques* (Paris: Calmann-Lévy, 1986), pp. 99–100.

The Abolition of Directive Planning

The new rules of the game introduced on January 1, 1968, rested thus on the elimination of both centralized production planning (that is, the disaggregation, or breaking down, of targets) and the administrative rationing of supplies. The annual plan that each enterprise had to draw up ceased to be a segment of a plan at a higher level; the enterprise was no longer compelled to submit its plan to the higher hierarchical echelon. Moreover, the reform established direct commercial contacts between the enterprise and its suppliers and customers. The national plan was thus no longer broken down hierarchically into plans for individual enterprises. The planners now sought to influence the enterprises through the intermediary of "regulators" of a general nature and not through detailed and individualized directives.

Even though the independence of enterprises remained constrained by administrative intervention, the NEM increased the enterprises' autonomy both qualitatively and quantitatively, beyond what had been accomplished in the experiments at systemic adjustment considered earlier. Two characteristics of the NEM should be underscored here. First was the relative and surprising ease with which it was implemented, a result doubtless of the amount of preparation and of the relative lack of macroeconomic tensions at the time of its introduction. Second, the changes introduced in 1968 were mutually reinforcing, so that despite the recentralization during the 1970s, Hungary never returned to mandatory planning or the central allocation of resources.

More Flexibility in Setting Prices

The place given to prices in the NEM illustrates the relative maturity of these reforms for the time. The general goal was to reduce the center's control over price determination and to reestablish a link between domestic and international prices so that market forces could gain some influence in price formation. The first change introduced might not seem all that unusual: the setting of less-irrational new wholesale prices in 1968, which would lead to fewer deviations in profitabilities. But the new administered structure was also established by taking prices on international markets into account (often the new price was a weighted average of the old domestic price and the price of a similar, imported product). Moreover, this resetting of wholesale prices was announced as the last of its type and would be applied only to some goods and services. In a manner quite similar to what happened in Czechoslovakia, four categories of prices were introduced in 1968—fixed, maximum, those with upper and lower limits, and free—with a stated goal of gradu-

Plan, Market, and Regulators

The key aspect of the reform of the economic mechanism is the combination of planned central management with commodity relationships and the active role of the market, based on social ownership of the means of production.

During the last few decades, extensive discussions have occurred among economists in the socialist countries about the role of commodity and monetary relationships in socialism. Most participants in this debate have rejected the argument that commodity relationships are incompatible with socialism and that we should only consider them as "necessary evils" and, for those reasons, that we should continue to limit them in order to eliminate them eventually. Instead, most economists have come to see that commodity relationships and the law of value exist and work effectively in a socialist system. In the interest of maximizing our progress, we should utilize them as much as possible. That means we must take advantage of commodity relationships and everything that comes along with them—the market, prices, costs of production, profits, credit, and so on—so that they play a larger and more active role in the socialist economy. ...

As our reform sees it, the role of the market would be quite different from its role under capitalism. We want a type of planned market relationship, rather than the spontaneous activity one finds in capitalism. Another basic difference is that labor will not become a commodity. Similarly, as far as enlarged reproduction is concerned, investment will not be a function of market situations but will be one of the intentionally planned goals set by the state, which will play a major role in determining the proper levels. ...

The enterprise is about to lose all mandatory planning goals. Does that mean that all the links between the state plan and the enterprise plan are going to be abolished? No, it won't be like that. In the future, the state's plan will still play a major role. But, it won't be the arbitrarily set indicators but the economic regulators that will define the relationship between the state and the enterprises. As efficient (if not more so) as the mandatory indicators, the regulators will be able to regulate total output and production levels, overall employment, expected growth in personal income, without being tailored to the output of any individual enterprise while, most important of all, taking longer-term concerns into account. Thus, the regulators will not "drop from the sky" each New Year's Day like the mandatory goals issued by the planners. The primary advantage will be that the regulators, while giving enterprises an incentive to operate efficiently within the state's economic policy, will not tie the hands of directors of enterprises in the effort to find the best way of using their productive capacity. Instead, they will force enterprise directors to begin thinking more in the long term.

Source: Interview with Reszö Nyers, Central Committee Secretary of the Socialist Workers Party of Hungary, *La réforme du mécanisme de l'économie en Hongrie* (Budapest: Editions Pannonia, 1969), pp. 9, 10, 13.

ally reducing the number of fixed-price goods. The first three categories were actually quite similar—the maximum or upper limit was generally used. The key was thus the introduction of free prices, which were supposed to be used for three-quarters of the wholesale prices for manufactured goods and almost one-quarter of the retail prices for consumer goods. Hopes for expanding the number of freely determined prices, given the very low initial inflation rates (less than 2 percent for retail prices during the first three years), were shattered during the 1970s when internal and external pressures led to stricter control over prices. The return, noticeable at that time, to a general rigidity, together with periodic revisions, should not keep us from seeing the importance of the initial flexibility or the relative reduction in the discrepancies in relative prices. Thus, during the 1970s, annual adjustments in the price of consumer goods were carried out administratively, most often with compensatory adjustments in wages as well.

The Regulation of Enterprise Revenues

The NEM sought to reduce and rationalize the redistribution process. Its architects hoped to do so by moving toward more uniform taxation of enterprises, which would allow them to keep a significant part of their profits and, as a result, motivate them to seek higher profits—and thus to improve their efficiency as well as to satisfy demand. The new prices introduced in 1968 included a tax of 5 percent on fixed and circulating capital. These uniform rates sent the enterprises a signal that, in principle, the state would no longer withhold an arbitrary share of their incomes. Nonetheless, taxes on production and profits introduced at the same time were designed to avoid profit levels that were too high and regulate the way retained profit was divided between bonuses and investment. The taxes demonstrated that the Hungarians were still far from "parametric" regulation. An important aspect of the reform was the noticeable reduction of the role of the turnover tax, which was also made more uniform (significant reduction in the number of rates, shift to a tax proportional to value [ad valorem] rather than an ad hoc tax), thereby permitting the reestablishment of a link between wholesale and retail prices. Once having paid the different taxes, the enterprise could keep what was left of its profit (as well as 60 percent of its depreciation funds). A set formula was then used to divide that money between an investment fund and a "sharing fund" that was used to pay bonuses.

A Very Limited Decentralization of Investment

In keeping with the radical reformist thought of the time, the state was to maintain its leading role in "enlarged accumulation." The center, thus,

Putting the Hierarchy of Control into Question

For Tamas Bauer, the elimination of the intermediary control organs between the ministry and the enterprises that was missing in Czechoslovakia in 1967 and Poland in 1982 was an essential element in the reformist "package" in 1968.

> I consider the abolishment of the comprehensive control hierarchy, of mandatory planning, and of centralized resource allocation to be the three basic components of the reform.
>
> Under perfectioning the economic mechanism the all-embracing control hierarchy has always been reshaped but maintained. The shift from the branch principle to territorial principle in the late fifties (USSR, Bulgaria) or the creation of large units with economic accounting (VVB in the GDR, VHJ in Czechoslovakia in the fifties and sixties, WOG in Poland in the seventies) or of minor and technologically more closed ones (*Kombinate* in the GDR and "concerns" in Czechoslovakia in the seventies and eighties) has never questioned the principle that all economic units constituted parts of one comprehensive hierarchy and continued to be administratively subordinated to the centre. Under the Hungarian NEM, the medium-level control agencies were liquidated, except if transformed into central managements of nation-wide enterprises. The remaining enterprises (nation-wide or not) were formally emancipated from the administrative subordination to the state administration (although their directors continued to be appointed etc. by the ministries up to now) [which] turned into genuine emancipation in respect of numerous small and medium-sized enterprises.

Source: Tamas Bauer, "Reforming or Perfectioning the Economic Mechanism," *European Economic Review* 31, nos. 1–2 (1987): 136.

continued to control the large investment projects, which it financed through the budget. The free allocation of funds was nonetheless progressively replaced by interest-bearing loans (this conversion was completed in 1976). For smaller-scale projects, the NEM allowed firms to make decisions on their own on a self-financing basis (retained profit) and by borrowing money from the bank. The role anticipated for bank lending was more limited than in Czechoslovakia; it was to include no more than 20 percent of total investment.

Five years after the reform, investment financed through the state's budget accounted for 47 percent of the total, self-financing 43 percent, and bank loans 10 percent. In reality, the informal centralization of supposedly "autonomous" finance remained high. Only 15 to 20 percent of the total was truly decentralized.

Wages and Employment

The changes introduced by the NEM for determining wages were gradual and complicated. The formal elimination of the traditional system in which the ministry determined the wages fund for each enterprise (notably by setting a ceiling for increases) and the decision that the firm should now earn the funds it needed for wages on its own touched one of the pillars of centralized planning. In reality, however, administrative intervention remained significant in this area through frequent changes in rules and in the taxation system. One must note, however, that, as was the case in many other areas, this type of administrative regulation became more indirect than direct. At first, the Hungarians introduced the regulation of average wages. This measure was significant because it tried to avoid unemployment, which the reform might logically have been expected to produce. During the debates before 1968, this point had been raised and the principle of full employment had been reaffirmed as strongly as possible. In setting the average wage centrally, the government gave firms the incentive to compensate for raising some workers' wages by reducing some others, thereby avoiding any layoffs or firings.

Beginning in 1971, gross income (profits plus wages fund) per employee became the success indicator used in evaluating firms. For each 1 percent of increased income, the base wage could be increased by 0.3 percent. The increase in the average wage was taxed at 50 percent (of the supplemental wage costs). Above the authorized limit, a progressive, supplementary tax (from 150 to 400 percent of the new wage costs) would be paid out of the wages fund.

These principles were designed to give the government new ways to block excessive wage increases. At the same time, the NEM gave man-

An Easing of the Monopoly on Foreign Trade

The reform also envisaged an increase in competitiveness due to changes in the system of foreign economic relations ... [in order] to bring down the wall separating domestic and foreign spheres of activity, which in the past had been the institutional counterpart of treating foreign operations as a residual element within an essentially autarkic orientation, especially with regard to the capitalist world. Its particular application can be set out as five measures: the replacement of physical targets in foreign-trade planning by guidelines and quotas in aggregate terms (although exchanges with other Comecon members presented formidable problems); a substantial increase in the number of domestic entities entitled to engage in foreign-trade operations ... ; the linking of prices in foreign-trade transactions (both import and export) and domestic prices through the official exchange rate coefficient (with the limits discussed above); a greater use of tariffs differentiated by commodity and source to dampen the propensity to import; and the extension of various forms of industrial cooperation with Western firms (including, in 1970, permission for minority shareholding by foreign corporations).

Source: Wlodzimierz Brus, *Institutional Change Within a Planned Economy,* in M. Kaser, ed., *The Economic History of Eastern Europe,* vol. 3 (Oxford: Clarendon House, 1986), pp. 180–181.

The Continuing Problem of Investment

Decentralization in investment decisions and financing of enterprise investment from its own resources and bank credit did not heal the known diseases of investment activities. Though enterprises' decision making about investment increased (in the middle of the 1970s it amounted to 55 per cent) capital productivity did not improve. The screening of the investment projects (including the calculation of expected profitability in world market prices, which became more or less a formality) by the bank did not turn out to be an instrument of efficiency, and long-term bank credit was extended to investments preferred by the government. Investment activity grew at a greater rate than the economy could afford; because of the improper working of the reform, enterprises had more funds for investment than was assumed; on top of this investment activity was marked by quite large fluctuations. The reform with its inconsistencies was only part of the problem; the main "culprit" was the economic policy which still adhered to a great extent to the old strategy of economic growth.

Source: Jan Adam, *Economic Reform in the Soviet Union and Eastern Europe Since the 1960s* (London: Macmillan, 1989), p. 83.

agement more flexibility in setting employment levels and structure at the workplace. Moreover, the rules that had forced workers to remain with one enterprise were abolished, thus allowing mobility in the labor force.

Agriculture and the Private Sector

In Hungary, there were changes made outside the systemic core both before and during the implementation of the New Economic Mechanism, which was essentially based on the questioning of centralized planning.

Agriculture had been collectivized between 1959 and 1961 but was substantially reorganized in the middle of the 1960s. Freed from compulsory deliveries (after 1957) and then of mandatory plans (1966), the cooperatives gradually turned into what came close to commercial enterprises—always constrained, to be sure, by various forms of administrative intervention. In 1967, the purchase prices for agricultural goods were increased 17 percent. The cooperative nature of collective farms became less formal, and there was a reduction of the state's paternalistic attitude toward the sector as a whole. The importance and autonomy of family plots grew in 1967 when the authorities proclaimed that collective and family production should not be seen as contradictory but as part of a whole agricultural system. Above all, the encouragement given to nonagricultural auxiliary production by the collective farms had spectacular effects. Between 1968 and 1971, the industrial and the food-processing activities of the latter more than doubled, while construction increased two and one-half times. This diversification played an important role in the evolution of the Hungarian model of development. More generally, agricultural performance contributed to significant improvement in overall food supply.

During the prolonged process of reform and especially during the 1970s, both the formal and the informal parts of the private sector grew dramatically. Despite the many remaining restrictions on it, such as on the size of enterprises (limited to three to five persons other than family members during the 1960s and 1970s, and seven during the 1980s), the tolerance given to the private sector explains much of its dynamism. Its share of the service sector—restaurants, construction, small-scale retailing, automobile repair—became larger than in the other socialist economies. Although it remained a relatively small part of the overall economy, the private sector was a significant factor in the evolution of the general model of consumption and development that emerged in Hungary at the time. Its contribution to activating the role of money was also substantial.

Bonuses and Conflicts
over the Distribution of Income

The reformers believed that the success of the reform depended on managers and therefore made provisions for quite a large differentiation in bonuses. In order to make this differentiation more acceptable, it was combined with a reversed differentiation in wage (salary) guarantees. For the distribution of bonuses from the sharing fund, all employees of an enterprise were divided into three categories. In the first category, consisting of top managers, bonuses could amount to 80 per cent of their salaries (salary guarantee 75 per cent). Members of the second category (heads of departments, supervisors, engineers, etc.) were entitled to 50 per cent of their total salaries as a group (85 per cent salary guarantee). Blue-collar workers and others who made up the third group were limited to bonuses amounting to 15 per cent of earnings as a group (100 per cent wage guarantee). ...

This distribution of bonuses was very much resented by blue-collar workers not only for material reasons, but also because they saw in the system an act of discrimination against them. In addition, it introduced conflicts of interest as to the use of the sharing fund. Top managers were interested in using the sharing fund as much as possible for bonuses. From an increase in the amount of bonuses corresponding to 1 per cent of the wage bill, they themselves could expect an increase in salaries of 4–5 per cent, whereas blue-collar workers received only 0.7–0.8 per cent in earnings. ... Due to political pressure the authorities abolished the mentioned distribution of bonuses. In order to retain the incomes of top managers a new bonus was introduced and designed in a way that it would not conflict with interests of wage earners.

Source: Jan Adam, *Economic Reform in the Soviet Union and Eastern Europe Since the 1960s* (London: Macmillan, 1989), pp. 80–81.

Table 10.1   The Relative Size of the Second Economy (in percent)

	First Economy (State-owned Firms and Cooperatives)	Second Economy (Formal and Informal Private Sector)
Distribution of total active time (excluding time spent on household work and transport in 1984	67.0	33.0
Contributions of social sectors to residential construction (measured by the number of new dwellings) in 1984	44.5	55.5
Contribution of social sectors to repair and maintenance services in 1983	13.0	87.0

Source: Janos Kornaï, "The Hungarian Reform Process: Visions, Hopes, and Reality," *Journal of Economic Literature* 24 (Dec. 1986): 1714–1715 and 1707, table 6. Reprinted by permission.

Table 10.2   The Formal Private Sector (in thousands of people)

	1953	1955	1966	1975	1980	1984
Private craftsmen	51.5	97.6	71.3	57.4	63.7	76.1
Employees and apprentices of private craftsmen	4.0	16.0	26.7	19.7	20.1	26.9
Private merchants	3.0	9.0	8.5	10.8	12.0	22.4
Employees of private merchants	–	1.0	1.5	3.4	8.2	28.5
People working full-time in business work partnerships*	–	–	–	–	–	11.0
Total number of people working full-time in the formal private sector	58.5	123.6	108.0	91.3	104.0	164.9

*Business work partnership: small enterprise based on private ownership by the participants. Introduced at the beginning of the 1980s, this form is a mix of small cooperative and of small capitalist enterprise managed by the owner.

Source: Janos Kornaï, "The Hungarian Reform Process: Visions, Hopes, and Reality," *Journal of Economic Literature* 26 (Dec. 1986): 1705, table 5. Reprinted by permission.

The Impact of the New Economic Mechanism

At first glance, the graph of Hungarian growth seems to suggest that the NEM had a positive impact. Average annual growth of national income in real terms (net material product) went from 4.5 percent in the period 1961–1965 to 6.8 percent in 1966–1970 and 6.3 percent in 1971–1975, but it fell afterward to 3.2 percent in 1976–1980 and 1.3 percent in 1981–1985. However, this general pattern of growth was not much different from that of the other Eastern European countries, which did not adopt such

Different Economic Sectors:
Conflict and Coexistence

Hungary has a multisectoral economy; different forms of ownership coexist and compete with each other. But competition is on unequal terms. With some simplification we may speak about a preference ordering of the bureaucracy: 1. large state-owned firms, 2. small state-owned firms, 3. agricultural cooperatives, 4. non-agricultural cooperatives, 5. formal private sector, 6. informal private sector. [This ordering was followed in the handing out of credits. It was the case also—but less so—for the frequency of microinterventions by the administration, particularly in the realm of price and wage setting.]

There is a feeling of complementarity, but also a feeling of rivalry between the various sectors; and there are collisions between them. The sectors lower on the state's preference scale suffer because in many allocative processes regulated by the bureaucracy, they are "crowded out" by sectors higher on the scale. At the same time, the same lower-preference sectors may be successful in "crowding out" the favorites of the state in the competition on the market. The most important example [is] bidding for labor in short supply. ...

In short, the Hungarian economy is a symbiosis of a state sector under indirect bureaucratic control and a nonstate sector, market oriented but operating under strong bureaucratic restrictions. Coexistence and conflict exist between the social sectors in many ways and all the time.

Source: Janos Kornaï, "The Hungarian Reform Process: Visions, Hopes, and Reality," *Journal of Economic Literature* 24 (Dec. 1986): 1714–1715.

radical reforms. Rather, the gains made as a result of these reforms were mostly qualitative. For example, there was a clear improvement in the food supply and the variety of products available. More generally, shortages became less severe, especially for consumer goods, and those for agricultural products all but disappeared. Industrial productivity significantly increased and was the primary cause of growth in that sector.

The shift in the traditional development model, which had already started at the beginning of the 1960s, intensified. Overall, industrial growth slowed down, while it was speeding up in agriculture and the service sector. From then on, the consumer goods sector grew at a faster rate than that of production goods. The opening to other Eastern European and, especially, Western markets continued. The improvement in people's standard of living prompted a break with the old mode of consumption. Spending on housing, vacation homes (secondary residences), tourism, and cars, as well as the wider availability of these goods and services, had a stimulating effect on the search for higher incomes and on productivity. The beginnings of "fordism," the mass production and consumption regime based on productivity growth that characterized postwar development in the Western advanced economies, seemed to appear.

This shift was never achieved, however. The general tendencies and the forms of behavior common in a shortage economy were merely reduced.

The Slowdown in the 1970s

Between the end of 1972 and 1979, the pendulum swung back in the other direction for a number of reasons. A conservative counteroffensive was waged by what amounted to an interest group made up of the larger firms, the ministerial apparatus, local Party cadres, and the unions, which took advantage of the working-class dissatisfaction with the growing inequality in income. After 1969, Brezhnevite conservatives in the Soviet Union along with their colleagues in the Czechoslovak and East German Communist parties stepped up their criticisms of the Hungarian policies. Between 1973 and 1975, recentralization occurred also when the authorities tried to limit the destabilizing impact of the international economic crisis on the most open economy in Eastern Europe.

In November 1972, the Central Committee introduced "extraordinary measures," which declared that the country's fifty largest enterprises (covering 50 percent of industrial production, 60 percent of exports) would be subject to direct ministerial supervision. A large wage increase, paid primarily through the state budget, lobbied for by the unions but contrary to the principles of the NEM, was granted. Central

Reform and Social Compromise

The Hungarian reforms would not have lasted if their social repercussions since 1968 had not been limited. The comparison with Yugoslavia is significant in this respect. Full employment was always guaranteed in Hungary, whereas the number of people unemployed in Yugoslavia grew from 290,000 in 1971 to 540,000 in 1975 (despite the outlet provided by migration). In Hungary, the annual increase in retail prices reached a maximum of 5% in 1976 (compared to 24% in Yugoslavia the year before) before declining slightly in 1977 and 1978. The planned price increases for certain widely used consumer goods (milk, later meat) could be carried out without provoking a social explosion such as those Poland experienced in 1970, 1976, and 1980 because of a system of monetary compensation aimed at protecting purchasing power of the least well paid. ... The state kept sufficient control over the evolution of incomes to raise wages in "unproductive" sectors, develop a family policy (including a kind of salary for housewives, increasing allowances for children), and reduce the worst shortfalls in the pension system. The influence of the market, which had been such an important part of the thinking underlying the NEM, thus did not compromise the pursuit of basic social goals, which actually had been seriously neglected before the reform of 1968.

Source: Jean-Charles Asselain, *Plan et profit en économie socialiste* (Paris: Presses de la Fondation Nationale des Sciences Politiques, 1981), pp. 287–288.

control over prices was reinforced—and would be even more so after 1973—wiping out the logic of gradual liberalization promoted in 1968. During this period, the government decided to restrict some of the autonomy granted to agricultural cooperatives. An ideological campaign against consumerism and petit bourgeois "enrichment" gave new life to the egalitarian tradition and opposed "speculation." Reszö Nyers was removed from the Party Secretariat in November 1973 and from the Politburo the following year.

From 1976 on, recentralization continued. The room for maneuver that enterprises had enjoyed was reduced in a number of ways. The degree of central redistribution was increased, while direct and indirect intervention by the ministries was intensified.

However, freezing the reform process did not entirely end the New Economic Mechanism or take Hungary back to where it had been before 1968, as Tamas Bauer himself noted. This is a point worth noting; it will be extremely important when we consider Hungary's return to reformist policies after 1979.

The Turning Point: 1972

The return of groups and of conservative concepts from autumn 1972 on in actual fact froze the reformist process.

The "second stage" of the reform which had been planned and prepared for introduction in the 1970s was removed from the agenda. In other words, the brakes which had been temporarily built into the reform in 1968, as guarantees of a smooth and gradual transition, were not removed after all. So the consciously created ambivalence of the reform system solidified and what had been believed to be transitory by those initiating the reform now became rigid and strengthened the contradictions; this automatically reinforced the trends toward recentralization. In the absence of a consistently normative system of regulation, the exception-riddled regulations in force so to speak reproduced the command system in other ways. What is more, the modifications to the regulators, the strengthening of direct intervention, particularly in the case of the fifty largest industrial companies, the centralization of more of the company profits and the effort to make the cooperative farms more like the traditional Soviet *kolkhoz* crippled a reform system which had already been seriously weakened by compromise.

Source: Ivan T. Berend, *The Hungarian Economic Reforms: 1953–1988* (Cambridge: Cambridge University Press, 1990), p. 231.

Strong and Weak Points of the New Economic Mechanism

More than fifteen years after the reforms of 1968 were introduced, Laszlo Szamuely observed that the NEM amounted to a third model of a planned socialist economy in Hungary, along with the Soviet and Yugoslav ones. The innovations in the 1966 program and its impact after its implementation in 1968 are the following:

1. "A planned economy has been realized without detailed prescriptions, planned targets regarding volume and mix of goods on [the] part of the central bodies."
2. Shifting to trade in the means of production instead of the earlier allocation of machinery and material.
3. Economic pluralism (acceptance of different types of enterprises and forms of ownership). This is one of the original contributions of the 1966 program and the achievements of 1968 and was not found in any of the other socialist countries.
4. "The linking of external and internal markets."

The limitations and defects of the NEM were already present when the proposals were first made in 1966 and included the following:

1. Decision making and financing for investment remained under central control. The theoretical basis for this direction, already present in 1956–1957, was given in the book by Wlodzimierz Brus.
2. The maintenance of control agencies and their staff. The goal here was to avoid opposition to the reforms the ministerial apparatus.
3. The absence of a simultaneous reconsideration of overall economic policy or of the extensive economic growth strategy, which headed the economy toward quantitative measures of performance and left it essentially autarkic.
4. A "technocratic approach. … Since the reform conception essentially contained no ideas about the solution of the expected social tensions and troubles, when these actually emerged both the political and economic leadership and wider public opinion were caught unprepared."

Source: Adapted and excerpted from Laszlo Szamuely, "The Second Wave of Economic Mechanism Debate and the 1968 Reform in Hungary," *Acta Œconomica* 33, nos. 1–2 (1984): 58–63.

The Systemic Shift of the Hungarian Economy

Unlike the other Hungarian economists such as Janos Kornaï, who emphasized the continuities in the behavior and forms of regulation, before and after the introduction of the NEM, Tamas Bauer characterized the latter as a qualitative transformation of the system. The economic mechanisms of most of the countries were in more or less constant evolution. In Bulgaria, East Germany, or the Soviet Union, for example, there was an oscillation around the "equilibrium point," which was a more or less moderate version of the traditional model of central planning.

> The history of the New Economic Mechanism in Hungary can also be presented as that of "reform cycles." Just to recall: after its introduction and moderate advancement toward "market socialism" (but still very far from anything like that) a period of retreat followed in the early and mid-seventies. The early eighties constituted another period of movement in the direction of the reform blueprint, but this movement has already lost momentum by now. This is also a certain oscillation, but the "equilibrium point" is beyond the system of central planning in the "field" of the hybrid which I described as "neither plan nor market." ... In the Hungarian case, the departures from this "equilibrium point" in the direction of a "market socialist" system are limited, and the efforts to advance further always ended with retreats to that hybrid state—but not to the traditional system of central planning that Hungary abandoned in 1968. ...
>
> It was a reform as it constituted a move from one "equilibrium point" to another one.

Source: Tamas Bauer, "Reforming or Perfectioning the Economic Mechanism," European Economic Review 31, nos. 1–2 (1987): 135.

11 Modernization in China Under Deng Xiaoping (1979–1989)

The Chinese radical reforms of the 1980s should be interpreted in the light of the particular nature of the country's history following the revolution of 1949. China's society was, of course, a predominantly rural one, in which agriculture predominated and deeply influenced the political and economic evolution of the Communist regime. The size of the country was also a decisive factor from both a demographic and a geographic perspective. The difficulty of linking the center, regions, and local communities has been a constant throughout Chinese history. Only the former Soviet Union and Yugoslavia experienced anything like this structural tension. With regard to the system, two important events occurred in the mid-1950s. The first was a very systematic application of the Soviet model in industry in all but two respects—its introduction was more gradual (for example, nationalization), and industry's share of the economy as a whole was much smaller. Second, for several reasons, the collectivization of agriculture, carried out in 1955 and 1956, was less conflict ridden than in the other socialist countries. With the exception of the catastrophic Great Leap Forward and the fluctuations of weather and politics, growth in agricultural production in the collectivized farms remained at a respectable level for a country at China's stage of development.

Reformist Fluctuations During the Maoist Period

In 1956, Mao Zedong began criticizing the Soviet model of organization and development, and his criticisms became increasingly radical with the passage of time. The Soviet model did have powerful supporters in China, and the conflict between them and Mao became one of the key causes of the wide-scale political struggles that characterized the Maoist period in Chinese politics (1956–1976). Mao did share the Stalinist antipathy for the market. A series of original reform efforts, oscillating between systemic adjustments and non–market oriented radical reforms, were introduced under Mao's rule. But he had no intention of creating markets. The defining characteristic of this voluntarist model, which did

The Excesses of Ministerial Centralization

At present scores of hands are reaching out to the localities, making things difficult for them. Once a ministry is set up, it wants to have a revolution, so it issues its orders. Since the ministries don't think it proper to issue orders to the Party committees and people's councils at the provincial level, they establish direct contact with the relevant departments and bureaus in the provinces and municipalities and give them orders every day. These orders, which are all supposed to come from the central authorities, even though neither the Central Committee of the Party nor the State Council knows anything about them, put a great strain on the local authorities. There is such a flood of statistical forms that they become a scourge. This state of affairs must be changed.

Source: Mao Tsetung (Mao Zedong), "On the Ten Great Relationships," *Selected Works of Mao Tsetung,* vol. 5 (Beijing: Foreign Language Press, 1977), p. 293.

not attack the institutional base, was its combination of extensive administrative decentralization (regional and local) and the politicization of economic management or, more generally, of the use of ideological or political criteria to provide a sort of "coordination through mobilization."

The first reform in this direction came at the same time as the Great Leap Forward of 1958. People's communes, in certain respects amounting to a "supercollectivization," were formed, but this time they were met by strong peasant resistance. These new units (the communes), led by local Party cadres, absorbed the local administrative functions that had previously been separate from agricultural production. The policy led, not to the anticipated rapid growth, but to the economic catastrophe of 1959–1961, including the collapse of agricultural and industrial production and widespread famine. Through a corrective "readjustment" in the early 1960s, the scope of collectivization was sharply cut back, even though the formal structure of the communes remained while recentralizing administrative measures were being taken. However, this recentralization was never fully achieved. Several new thrusts toward decentralization took place, giving the well-known cycle of centralization–rigidity and stagnation–decentralization–disorder and confusion–recentralization.

During the Cultural Revolution, the Maoist search for a third way, as different from the Stalinist model as from the systemic adjustments and radical reforms in Eastern Europe (denounced as the "restoration of capitalism"), gained new support. Attempts were made to change enterprise management (with the slogan "politics takes command"), but no consistent systematic or organizational alternative was formulated by the radicals, who ended up losing once and for all. The innovations were easiest to see in development strategy (for example, the extension of rural industry) and in the slogan of "self-reliance," which implied an autarkic attitude not only on the national, but also on the regional and even microeconomic, levels. The development of a "cellular economy" seemed to make sense given this antimarket orientation, administrative decentralization, and the weakness of the Chinese transportation network. It also allowed for the easing of bottlenecks and other problems associated with a centralized supply system.

Rural Reform and Decollectivization

The Chinese leadership's reformist orientation under Deng Xiaoping (beginning in 1978) has been most clearly marked by an economic pragmatism, sustained by a public weariness after years of factional struggle, and a deliberate strategy of limiting political change that might under-

The Decentralized Administrative Socialism of 1958

The main reform measures adopted in 1958 were the following:

1. The great majority of central ministry enterprises were transferred to local control.

2. In production planning, the system of unified balance achieved through the State Planning Commission was transformed into one based on regional planning and bottom-to-top balancing. The number of products under the control of the State Planning Commission was greatly reduced, and local authorities were granted important planning and allocative powers.

3. In investment planning, a subcontracting system was adopted: the central authorities distributed funds to the local authorities, who added their own funds and then chose investment projects on their own.

4. Reforms reduced the amount and the categories of materials inventories distributed by the State Planning Commission and the ministries, leaving the rest to be distributed by local government. The local authorities could reallocate centrally rationed materials to enterprises in their region, including central ministry enterprises, and could also share in the surplus output produced by local enterprises.

5. The financial system was sharply decentralized: taxes were assigned to provincial governments for collection, with various tax retention rates, fixed for five years. Meanwhile, the central government gave the power to reduce, exempt, or increase a tax to the local authorities.

6. The former highly centralized credit system was replaced by "delegating credit control to lower levels and controlling only the debit-credit differential."

Source: Wu Jinglian, "The Evolution of Socialist Economic Theories and the Strategic Options of Reform in China," in K. Dopfer and K.-F. Raible, *The Evolution of Economic Systems: Essays in Honour of Ota Sik* (London: Macmillan, 1990), p. 267.

mine the regime's legitimacy. The leaders' principal desire has been to "modernize" the country and spark a rapid economic takeoff, while leaving the system's institutional base intact. The leaders still referred to the system as "socialist," but it became harder and harder to tell what they meant by that.

Agriculture was the first area of reforms, with the people's communes under ever-increasing criticism. The Maoists had stressed that these vast collective organizations played a major role in building up the agricultural infrastructure, improving the health and life expectancy of the rural population, and expanding primary education and other cultural and social services (in addition to their functions for social control through the apparatus). After Mao's death, the reformers questioned the confusion among the political, economic, and administrative leadership and, above all else, the weakness of material incentives for peasants in the collective-farm system. They went on to point out that during the 1960s and 1970s, agricultural production did not outpace population growth, leaving per capita food consumption stagnant.

Beginning in 1979 and, even more in 1981, the leadership began the transition to the "household responsibility system." A number of methods were used to redistribute communal land to groups or families who signed delivery contracts with production teams (collectives) and obtained real autonomy in the way they managed and organized their work. There was some initial resistance from rural cadres, but the new organizations gained a considerable degree of legitimacy by dramatically increasing production (which was stimulated as well by increased state prices for agricultural products). Then, peasant pressure forced ever more rapid decollectivization and the elimination of the commune system altogether in 1983 and 1984 (there was a record harvest that year). The new arrangements can be called family farming (land is assigned on the basis of fifteen-year leases, sometimes longer), with rent paid to the state as specified in contracts. Whatever was produced above and beyond those contracted amounts was kept by the family, who could consume or sell the surplus on the free market. In 1985, the state canceled all mandatory deliveries and, at the same time, the higher prices for goods sold above those quotas.

Until the middle of the 1980s, the "rural reforms" seemed to be a great success. Their negative effects, such as damage to the agricultural, health, and environmental infrastructure, social polarization, and a less-effective policy of birth control, seemed minor given the strong growth of production and income in the countryside. The excess labor cast free by decollectivization was largely absorbed in the private and "collective" sector under the control of local authorities; its very rapid expansion partially explains the increase (and also the destabilization) of overall

Mao Against the Traditional System and the Market

In the early 1960s, three different tendencies were visible, combining and conflicting in various ways.

The central, administrative planning approach of the "command economy," inherited from the Soviet Union, was in the defensive position. During the Cultural Revolution, it would come to be identified with Liu Shaoqi ..., then Chief of State. Its structural defenders were the political and administrative cadres whose careers it legitimized. In one opposing corner there was the "market socialism" option, propounded most eloquently by the economist Sun Yefang. Mao opposed both of these paths. The first he saw as unwieldy and ineffective economically, and as giving rise to a class of bureaucratic rulers, divorced from the masses politically. The second played to bourgeois values, opposing the socialist values of co-operation and solidarity in favour of individualism and profit orientation. Mao's goal, instead, was an economy that centralized control only of major macroeconomic variables and of the large-scale modern industries that he regarded as the "backbone" of the economy. Other activities would be the province of the regions and localities, using technologies appropriate to their sizes and resource bases and adopting the policy of "self-reliance."...

The Maoist response took on a quality of messianic irrationality that led to major disasters and ultimately compromised its own credibility. In retrospect, its weaknesses and failures can be seen to be due in part to problems intrinsic in the "logic" of the approach itself, and in part to intractability of the social conditions in which the approach was tried—if such a distinction can be made with validity.

Source: Carl Riskin, *China's Political Economy* (New York: Oxford University Press, 1987), pp. 82 and 84.

Table 11.1 Agricultural Production and Chinese Peasant Income in 1977–1988 (in millions of tons)

	Grains	Cotton	Oil Seeds	Red Meat	Per Capita Income[1]	Index of Per Capita Income[2]
1977	283	1.98	4.0	7.8	125	
1978	316	2.17	5.2	8.6	134	100
1979	332	2.21	6.4	10.6	160	117
1980	321	2.71	7.7	12.1	191	132
1981	325	2.97	10.2	12.6	223	150
1982	355	3.60	22.8	13.5	270	179
1983	287	4.64	10.6	14.0	310	202
1984	407	6.26	11.9	15.4	355	225
1985	379	4.15	15.8	17.6	398	232
1986	392	3.54	14.7	19.2	424	233
1987	405	4.25	15.3	19.9	463	237
1988	394	4.20	13.2	21.9	545	235

[1]In current yuan.
[2]In real terms.
Note: This table brings to the light the large increase in agricultural production and real income per capita until 1984 and the far less dramatic growth thereafter.
Source: Claude Aubert, "La crise agricole en Chine," *Le Courrier des Pays de l'Est*, no. 344 (Nov. 1989): 52.

growth during the 1980s. By 1988, 67 million people were employed in rural industry.

Urban and Industrial Reform

Encouraged by the evolution of agriculture, the reformist leaders introduced "urban reform" in 1984. State-owned industry was still largely run along Soviet lines, although not as rigidly: less centralization or "tautness" from the plan, and so forth. After 1978, several experiments of a more or less wide-scale nature had simplified administrative structures, limited the number of compulsory indicators, authorized various forms for retaining profits, or permitted autonomous production above and beyond the plan's quotas (this last point creating a situation analogous to the "responsibility system" in agriculture). Beginning in 1984, the reformist strategy was based on a dual model, supposed to be a mechanism for a gradual transition to a mixed system combining the plan (mandatory and indicative) with the market. In the new system, each enterprise's output would be broken into two parts: one planned according to traditional methods and the other outside the plan and determined autonomously (or, in some cases, through the indicative part of the plan). The leadership expected that this two-tiered system would gradually expand the size of the market while reducing the role of cen-

Centralization and Fragmentation
After the Great Leap Forward

As in agriculture, the state in the early 1960s attempted to restore many of the features of the pre–Great Leap system, but with one important modification. Planning based on physical input and output targets and the state-run material allocation system was restored, but no longer was all planning and allocation to be done by Beijing. Instead, many planning and allocation decisions were decentralized to the province and later even to the county. Provinces in China have an average population of 30 to 40 million and some approach 100 million or more. In many cases, enterprises obtained most of their inputs from within the province and most of their output was sold to others in the same province; hence there was no need to coordinate these inputs and outputs on a nationwide basis. By the 1970s a large proportion of Chinese enterprises were under the authority of the provinces rather than Beijing. In most cases, particularly with larger enterprises in strategic sectors, Beijing retained effective control even if planning formally was at the provincial level.

Source: Dwight H. Perkins, "Reforming China's Economic System," *Journal of Economic Literature* 26, no. 2 (June 1988): 606–607.

tral planning. One must note that the procedures for supply (guaranteed or autonomous) and for price setting (fixed or free) were also split between the two types of management.

Given the rapid growth in the 1980s, this two-tiered regime of production and prices had conflicting effects. On the one hand, it contributed to the rapid expansion of the independent market sector of the Chinese economy, with its "virtuous circle" of growth in the state industries' production beyond the plan's quotas and the development of agriculture and the urban and rural private and cooperative sectors. On the other hand, it helped create strong speculative and even corrupt practices. Enterprise managers speculated with the various supply channels and the two-tiered price system (for the same goods), thus finding an easy way to enrich themselves, which also proved to be the case for people at many levels of the administrative apparatus who started turning their activities into businesses.

The transformation of the wage labor system was an equally important goal of urban reform. Unlike the other socialist countries, China had kept the central allocation of the work force in the state sector, which meant no free movement of labor and a system of lifetime employment (often hereditary) from the 1950s on. The reforms set out to eliminate the strongly egalitarian wage structures and break the guaranteed employment of the "iron rice bowl." In reality, the results were mixed. The rise in bonuses permitted by the increase in the level of retained profit did not lead to a sharp differentiation in workers' wages because of the complicity between the workers and managers in favor of a rather egalitarian distribution. After 1986 a system of contract hiring for set periods—the former wage earners were kept on—was developed, but it remained relatively limited within the central core of state industries, with the exception of a precarious and marginal section of the work force that was part of the new urban underclass in the 1980s.

The Open-Door Policy

As early as the 1970s, the Chinese leadership had rejected the previous autarkic policies. That rejection, along with the urban reforms, led to a series of important institutional changes and a policy of export promotion. The monopoly on foreign trade was gradually weakened. Provinces, new corporations specializing in foreign trade, and existing enterprises were given the right to establish direct contacts with foreign partners and were allowed to keep part of the foreign currency they earned through exports. China joined the World Bank and International Monetary Fund, which gave it the opportunity to borrow funds on the world financial market. A flood of legislation authorizing mixed-capital

Privatization and the System of Rural Leases

Above and beyond the sale of agricultural capital belonging to the communes (livestock, mechanical equipment: tractors, cultivators) to families, collective ownership of land, while maintained in principle, changed in practice.

> After decollectivization, something very different from the "cooperative economy" the authorities still talked about was created. It amounted to a generalized lease-holding system with two levels of property rights. Teams (or villages where teams had disappeared), the legal owners of collective lands, received what could be called rent from the incomes of the families who had been allocated the land. In effect, the economic role of teams was reduced, and the liquidation or the placing in managerial hands of collectively owned wealth meant that the payments served essentially to maintain the village administration, representing the collective ownership of the land. Moreover, the families who had been allocated land and held long-term leases of fifteen years or more acted as if they were "owners" of the right to use the land; this right had to be paid for when it was transmitted to other persons. Almost all transmissions of contracts thus required the payment of a "compensation" by the benefiting family to the one that ceded its rights, though temporarily. Such arrangements were typically made for a year or two.

Source: Claude Aubert, "Les réformes agricoles ou la genèse incertaine d'une nouvelle voie chinoise," *Revue Tiers-Monde* 27, no. 108 (Oct.-Dec. 1986): 733.

or entirely foreign-owned companies was passed during the 1980s. Special Economic Zones (SEZ), in fact specializing in exports, were created in the Southeast. In 1984, fourteen big coastal cities were opened to foreign trade—many of them former "concessionary" cities, which had extraterritorial rule in pre-Communist days—followed by the three "development triangles" on the seacoast in 1985. By then, virtually the entire coastline, which included the most industrialized part of the country with the best infrastructure, had been opened to the Pacific Rim, with its Chinese diaspora, and to the world as a whole.

In conjunction with urban reform, opening the economy had spectacular results, introducing more competition, but also adding to speculation and corruption. In barely a decade, exports tripled (reaching 13 percent of GNP in 1988) and included mostly manufactured goods, while imports quadrupled. China's foreign trade went from 14 percent to nearly 28 percent of GNP between 1981 and 1989.

A Tendency Toward Economic Balkanization

The gradual, systemic changes that grew out of the many reforms of the 1980s were accompanied by an extensive redistribution of power and income on the social, regional, and sectoral levels. In particular, the power of regional and local authorities was reinforced at the expense of national ones.

Regional protectionism slowed down the "decompartmentalization" of the economy and the creation of a competitive national market. Each province erected its own barriers in an attempt to limit the competition of its neighbors, especially with respect to profitable consumer goods, or in order to conserve scarce resources, such as primary goods produced locally.

The Weakening of Macroeconomic Control

The central government had trouble in achieving efficient—to use a Chinese term—"macroregulation" after replacing the old methods of administrative control. Regional authorities saw their power in fiscal and budgetary matters reinforced. Together, these factors were major causes of overinvestment and the overheating of the economy in general in the second half of the 1980s. Growing macroeconomic pressures led to an inflationary thrust and an increased rate of accumulation, which was already very high. These drifts were facilitated by the newly decentralized and diversified banking system, operated under considerable local political pressure. Lacking the "fine-tuning mechanisms" of a central bank, the decentralized system tended to grant large loans with easy repay-

An Economy with Three Sectors

The White Paper of October 1984 called for an economy in which three forms of coordination would coexist and evolve: directive planning, indicative planning using economic levers, and market regulation.

First, our country has in general a planned economy, that is, a commodity economy governed by the plan and not an economy entirely subject to the regulating role of the market. Second, production and trade of one part of agricultural goods and auxiliary activities and of small articles for daily consumption, as well as services or repairs, are domains that are left exclusively to regulation by the market. These sectors of activity play a secondary role that is nonetheless indispensable in our national economy. Third, the use of a planned economy does not mean that mandatory plans constitute the principal element, because like the indicative ones, mandatory plans are but one of various concrete forms used in such an economy. Fourth, indicative plans will be achieved above all through the use of economic levers, whereas mandatory plans must be carried out in an obligatory manner, without ignoring the law of value. In conformity with the points mentioned above, reform of the current planning system will require a methodical and appropriate reduction in the areas in which directive planning operates and an appropriate expansion of indicative planning. In effect, directive planning will be used only for products of vital importance both for the national economy and for the life of our population and that are distributed in a uniform manner by the state, as well as for activities in the national interest. The numerous other products and economic activities can be included in the indicative plans or left entirely to regulation by the market on a case-by-case basis.

Source: "Décision du Comité central du P.C.C. sur la réforme du système économique,"
Beijing Information, no. 44 (Oct. 29, 1984): vi–vii.

Table 11.2 Key Materials Allocated by the State, According to the State Planning Commission Statistics (in percent)

	1979	1984	1988
Steel	77.0	66.0	46.8
Timber	85.0	40.0	25.9
Coal	58.9	50.0	43.5
Cement	35.7	25.0	13.6

Source: World Bank, China: Between Plan and Market (Washington: World Bank, 1990), p. 61, table 4.1.

ment plans far too freely. The center could not establish a genuine monetary policy. Instead, it had to step in periodically using crude across-the-board policies to slow down the expansion of credit by trying to recentralize fiscal policy again. This created a kind of reform cycle reminiscent of the investment cycle typically found in the traditional socialist economies.

After the strong inflationary push of 1985–1987, the government pursued a policy of strict austerity at the end of 1988, followed by a freeze on reform (and a purge of reformist leaders) after the massacre in Tiananmen Square in 1989. Nevertheless, after ten years of radical reform in the Chinese economy, many changes were irreversible.

A Planning System Falsely Labeled "Indicative"

Several general lessons can be drawn from a study of the coastal province of Zhejiang during the 1980s.

First, the guidance target was invariably linked to the provision of specific inputs to individual producers. Second, the absence of a stable definition of guidance planning is shown by the tendency for certain products subject to guidance planning to either revert to mandatory planning or evolve to full-market regulation. Third, local governments played an important role in promulgating guidance plans. While the central government used various instruments to shape local government incentives, particularly as they related to investment decisions, local governments in turn steered enterprises through a variety of mandatory and guidance instruments. Chinese guidance planning is clearly not a form of indicative planning that affects local unit behavior primarily through provision of information, nor does it shape local unit incentives by impartially altering relative prices. Instead, guidance planning is a general name for a set of ad hoc interventions by planners into new market arenas, using familiar instruments of material supply. Chinese guidance planning is unlikely to be more than a transitional form in the overall process of economic reform.

Source: Barry Naughton, "China's Experience with Guidance Planning," *Journal of Comparative Economics* 14, no. 4 (1990): 759.

The Perverse Effects of a Two-Tier Price System

The expansion of the market brought with it an explosion in the number of commercial state firms, which grew from 103,000 in 1978 to 327,000 in 1988, while the number of industrial firms only grew from 84,000 to 99,000. But the status of these commercial firms is by no means clear. They are often para-public companies, even fictitious companies, speculating on the differences between official and market prices. ...

As for the bureaucratic distribution networks, they have a de facto monopoly, deducting heavy commissions on non–plan based transactions, diverting a growing part of planned production to sell it at the higher market prices. Thus, the bureaucratic networks' grip on the market eliminates the search for equilibrium prices, giving over economic activity to speculation.

Source: Guilhem Fabre, "La Chine gangrenée par le mercantilisme du pouvoir," *Le Monde diplomatique,* Dec. 1990, p. 23.

The "Fief" Economy

Whereas, according to the book of reform, the economic role of governments will be one of "indirect control" (through the market) and "macro-regulation," the evidence shows that at the local level they have been increasingly involved in managing the economy. The reform has strengthened their profits and they "almost unavoidably" thrive on the few new powers granted by the Centre while arrogating to themselves the new powers that had been granted to the enterprises.

In practical terms, local governments fund new enterprises and very often decide on the upgrading of older ones. Whereas they are meant to keep a tight rein on the investment of fixed assets, they actually keep pushing for more investments. They mobilize the treasury, goods and materials, commerce and foreign trade departments; now that the banks have been placed under their control, they instruct bank managers to give loans to enterprises and enlarge the scope of investments, totally oblivious of the ensuing disruption to the economy.

Source: "Regional Protectionism," *China News Analysis,* Hong Kong, no. 1418 (Sept. 15, 1990): 5.

Part Four

Toward the Dismantling of the System

The dismantling of the socialist system in its traditional or reformed form has taken place when qualitative changes occurred not only in planning or in other components but also in its institutional base. The elimination of the single-party regime constitutes the ultimate criterion for the dismantling of the system because it is precisely the combination of this political arrangement with state ownership that makes up the institutional base. Thus, the revolutions that swept Eastern Europe in 1989 or the ban on the CPSU following the failed coup in 1991 in the USSR in a way eliminated the cornerstone of socialist systems. A tipping of the balance between the state and private sectors to the benefit of the latter could also have led to the dismantling of the system, even if the single-party political system had been maintained. But in this book, we are concerned with actual historical experiences and not abstract possibilities of systemic dismantling.

During the 1980s, the reformers' goals evolved from radical reform to the transformation of the system itself. We will start by considering that gradual shift. Then, we will discuss some significant experiences of dismantling. There is no way that we can cover them all in detail, and thus I will not include material on Czechoslovakia, Bulgaria, or Romania. Even though the point can be debated, I put Yugoslavia after the mid-1960s in this category of countries that went through intersystemic change. The more obvious cases of Poland and Hungary will be considered below, along with the GDR since German reunification.

12 The Evolution of Reformist Ideas During the 1980s

Although the views of economists who supported radical economic reforms hardly changed after the wave of reform in the 1960s, a new maturation occurred during the 1980s, especially toward the end of the decade. The shift from a strategy of reform to one favoring the dismantling of the socialist system and the transition to a market economy represents a fundamental change in their basic orientation and is vital to an understanding of the upheavals in Central and Eastern Europe since 1989.

From Optimism to Pessimism

The evolution of reformist ideas often went unnoticed at the time because it occurred gradually and because of the reformers' prudence. Nonetheless, it can be explained by a number of factors that came together and reinforced each other during the course of this critical decade. Obviously, the structural economic crisis that the Soviet Union and the Eastern European countries went through played a decisive role. That crisis occurred at the end of a long-term decline in growth, noticeable since the 1960s. It became harder and harder to believe in the superiority or even of the potential superiority of the socialist system over its capitalist rivals as an impetus for economic development. Until the 1980s, *optimism about the system* was found not only in official ideology (which had become nothing more than rhetoric) but also in the enlightened thoughts of the reformers who remained critical of capitalism as a system. During the 1980s, many of those reformers went through an ideological conversion following systemic disappointment, and that optimism was transformed into *pessimism about the system,* including the idea that socialism had reached a historical impasse. All the virtues that social tradition or state dogma had given it—at least as potentialities—were now transferred to its capitalist rival, including economic dynamism and the satisfaction of social needs.

119

A General Change in Attitude Toward the Market Economy

In a study of many Solidarity leaders and activists carried out during the summer of 1988, Wojciech Arkuszewski observed:

> The profound changes that occurred in people's minds during these last few years cannot be reduced to the impact of Solidarity alone but are the result of a larger crisis. I think about the vogue, all but universally accepted, of economic liberalism, which reigns on both sides of the political barricades and which finds support in the opposed political camps. This fashion divides the power elite and provokes strong resistance within the apparatus by putting its ideology into question and suggesting that it should give up any pretenses of running the economy. At the same time, it paralyzes Solidarity because if its activists think that one has to introduce market-based reforms, increase what is demanded of workers, and accept unemployment—all this is profoundly at odds with its role as a union. Solidarity thus makes ambiguous declarations and, de facto, defends people's standards of living very weakly. In this growing infatuation with economic liberalism, I do not see any place for the trade union Solidarity.

> [Leopolita (the pseudonym of a journalist) declared:] Solidarity actually was the last great revisionist movement in Poland. It accepted de facto the basic elements of a socialist economy because it had been convinced that one could make it work well as long as there were no more communists left. But since it wasn't possible to get rid of them, it was necessary to limit their power. In reality, this was not a program of reform or of a radical change of the regime. And this is exactly what changed in the aftermath of December 13, 1981. In people's minds, in the way they felt about things, the market economy had been rehabilitated. Until recently, such notions as "private initiative" and "private plot farming" had a pejorative meaning for many people. All this changed dramatically, and I believe that this new mind-set was one of the most important successes following the imposition of martial law, because people now saw that it was time to throw the entire socialist model out. This rediscovery of the private sector and the market left Solidarity's position as a union in a paradoxical situation.

Source: "Enquête en Pologne: Que reste-t-il de *Solidarité*?" *La Nouvelle Alternative,* no. 12 (Dec. 1988): 30–31.

The ultimate failure of the reforms attempted during the 1980s in Eastern Europe played a major role in this conversion to capitalism, which, once it came out into the open, astonished the West and delighted its free-marketeer economists. In Poland, for instance, the people rejected not only the traditional socialist model but eventually also any type of reformed socialism. The radicalization of reformist economists and other opposition figures thus was part of a far deeper social change.

The Impact of Theory

A book by Hungarian Janos Kornaï, *The Economics of Shortage*, published in 1980, influenced economic thought in the 1980s in many respects. Analyzing the traditional unreformed socialist system, it documented the systemic coherence that united its institutions, the behavior of economic agents, and shortages as general and chronic phenomena in consumption, the production of intermediate goods, and the work force. According to Kornaï, this type of economy had certain characteristics that were in a way the opposite of those of capitalism. Capitalism is based on a "hard budget constraint" (the behavior of firms depends on their monetary and financial resources), and the economy is constrained by demand (monetary) and marked by underemployment. In contrast, socialism is based on a "soft budget constraint," and the economy is constrained by physical resources and suffers from shortages.

This theory of an economy of shortages was also supported by the works of other members of the Hungarian school, such as the theory of the investment cycle developed by Tamas Bauer, which exposed the structural nature of the chronic tensions and the role of the "institutional-behavioral" complex in the regulation of socialist systems. The dysfunctionalities observed in the system were still frequently being explained in terms of planning errors or an overambitious growth policy; such explanations thus lost much of their influence. But the old approach based on radical reforms, with its continued optimism about the system (a reformed socialist economy would avoid the defects of the traditional model as well as those of the capitalist system), also found itself weakened.

A Self-Critical Balance Sheet

At the end of the 1970s, many reformist economists still thought that radical reform had failed largely because it had not been tested adequately or that (as in Hungary) it had been reined in for social and political reasons. In the early 1980s, new ideas about the limits of the reformist model itself came to the fore. In the ensuing debate, a critical evaluation

An Affirmation of Defeat for Radical Reforms

During a conference held in Vienna in November 1988, Leszek Balcerowicz concluded his study of Polish reforms during the 1980s as follows:

> The Polish case shows (as does the Hungarian) that one can move from comprehensive directive planning without introducing a market mechanism. The experience with such intermediate systems is not very encouraging. But this should not be interpreted as meaning that the efficiency-enhancing economic reform is to be sought in perfecting a system based on such planning. Attempts of this type are, in the author's view, futile. What the Polish experience shows is, rather, that a move from such a system must be more radical.

Source: Leszek Balcerowicz, "Polish Economic Reform, 1981–1988: An Overview," Economic Commission for Europe, *Reforms in the European Centrally Planned Economies* (New York: United Nations, 1989), p. 48.

Institutional Owners in the Public Sector?

Preoccupied with the establishment of an "owner's motivation" for state capital, as well as a better allocation of it in the various sectors, Marton Tardos made the following proposal in 1982:

> In the sphere of state ownership the supervision of enterprises should be exercised by 4–10 independently operating organizations. These capital owner, profit oriented holdings operating without limitations could successfully protect the enterprises in the competitive sphere from the hidden restoration of the hierarchic power structure and could successfully introduce the evaluation and supervision of enterprise activities on the basis of long-term profitability criteria. This form may provide ways for the reallocation of capital according to profit motives. The institution of "capital holders," perhaps complemented by banks, trade unions, insurance companies, would be authorized to close enterprises, to found new ones, to reallocate assets for the development of existing enterprises on the basis of expectable profits. The source of capital-reallocation could be, for example, the dividend paid by the enterprises to the owner organizations. The capital-holding organizations could thus accomplish the task, so far unresolved under socialist conditions, of reallocating capital, especially if their activities were complemented by the right to found subsidiaries.

Source: Marton Tardos, "Development Program for Economic Control and Organization in Hungary," *Acta Œconomica* 28 (1982): 307.

of the Hungarian experience after 1968 (a point we will return to later) played a central role.

Brus's model, which had inspired most radical reforms until then, differentiated between "current decisions" affecting "simple reproduction," which should be left to the enterprises, and the investment decisions touching "enlarged reproduction," which to a significant extent should be made by the center. The underlying argument was that the market is a weak mechanism for determining or reaching long-term goals. Only a rational and enlightened central authority could make adequate decisions in this respect. It was this hypothetical cleavage between market and plan that was to be put into question during the 1980s. It appeared that the central economic administration was not limiting itself to controlling investment but naturally tended to extend its authority to supposedly autonomous decision making, even in the absence of production planning, as was seen in Hungary after 1968. Moreover, the independence of the enterprise and its search for profit were blocked as growth and technical change were divorced from profitability, because above all else, profitability depended mainly on redistribution and bargaining with the administration. Once the economists reached this conclusion, they saw just how unrealistic their initial hypothesis separating the center and the enterprises in making investment decisions had been.

Capital Markets

Another new argument, developed primarily by the Hungarian Marton Tardos, strengthened the criticism of the model combining planning and a regulated market. Tardos claimed that there was an essential contradiction in limiting the market to products and not extending it to labor and capital. As a result, the market for products itself was weakened, and it was impossible to achieve the kind of "parametric regulation" envisioned in the NEM.

There was an obvious link between the continued centralization of a major part of investment and the need to maintain a powerful central administration. Moreover, the fact that capital could be reallocated between branches and regions only through central redistribution led to some unwanted and, indeed, perverse consequences. Because enterprises could not diversify their activities, they tended to push internal investment. The center, which had its own version of what the efficient allocation of investment funds meant, reacted by trying to reduce the enterprises' decision-making autonomy. Capital was frozen in a rigid structure. Changes were made only when the central authorities decided to open new branches or as a result of a struggle among sectoral

The New Liberalism

From Tibor Liska, professor of economics at Karl-Marx University in Budapest and disciple of Milton Friedman, to Miroslaw Dzielski, leader for the ultraliberals in Krakow, the new wave of liberals were shaped by their unshakable faith in the market (even though it did not work perfectly in the West) and their allegiance to the liberal Vienna School (Hayek, von Mises, etc.) and its extension, the Chicago School. It wasn't totally an accident that it was in Krakow, Budapest, or Prague that people began to draw on the Vienna school of thought, which had focused its critical analyses on the growth of state intervention and economic nationalism in the Austro-Hungarian Empire. It was not a question of nostalgia but an understanding that the disintegration of the Central European economic space and the triumph of state intervention meant that Central Europe had traveled farther down what Hayek had called the "road to serfdom." It was not only a question about a type of economy but also a choice between types of societies: an "open" economy was the first step toward an "open society." ...

It would be a mistake to think that partisans and adversaries of the market were divided logically as a function of their belonging to the state apparatus or to society. In fact, as the Hungarian sociologist Elemer Hankis pointed out, the dividing line passed through the two camps. The introduction of the market, of course, threatened the *nomenklatura* first, but it also put the implicit social contract between the latter and the working class ("you pretend to work, and we pretend to pay you") into question. The increased opportunity for freedom that the introduction of the market represented was proportional to the degree of insecurity that it implied for the labor market and incomes. From there emerged a conservative reflex, above all among the workers in the most subsidized sectors of the economy.

Source: Jacques Rupnik and Pierre Kende, "Libéralisme et crise du système communiste en Europe de l'Est," *L'Autre Europe,* nos. 15–16 ("Renouveau libéral à l'Est?") (1988): 9–10.

lobbyists. There was no way that shifts in domestic or international demand could be followed by rapid changes in the goods produced through the initiative of either existing or newly created firms. Finally, the beneficial effects of competition on technical progress or the quality of manufactured goods were blocked by the combination of a high concentration of industry and the absence of any mechanisms to reallocate capital among the various product lines.

Tardos's analysis led to an interpretation close to that of the general equilibrium model: The rationality of a market economy is derived from the interaction between the product, labor, and capital markets. Such interaction was missing in the radical reform model (for example, the NEM). This rediscovery of a classical argument from the Western liberal school of thought was accompanied by the gradual return of a concept that had been missing from the reformers' debates until that time, property.

Property and the Control of Capital

The question of property and ownership reappeared during the 1980s even in the reforms adopted by some of the incumbent governments (Poland and Hungary). The first approach was still timid and amounted to a shift from the idea of state ownership to a concept of a public sector run by representatives specifically or juridically defined in order to limit the blurring of property rights (in state or "social" ownership). The second and more radical approach was, in fact, a consequence of the attention paid to capital markets. If they were to be developed, state ownership itself would have to be "fragmented" to introduce more "fluidity" into the system. But here another argument developed by several reformers came into play. Earlier reforms had had many more real and beneficial effects outside the state sector than inside it (especially in countries like Hungary or China). Thus, at the beginning of the 1980s, a common reformist theme was to agree that it made sense to accept multiple forms of ownership, which permitted the expansion of a new private sector. By the end of the decade, some were ready to make an even more radical recommendation. The bearer of formal ownership should be changed. The state sector should be privatized.

The Wind from the West

This radicalization of an important portion of the economic community was in many respects an echo of the Western neoclassical theory of "property rights" that affirmed that the power of managers rather than owners (stockholders) was the source of inefficiency in capitalism and

From Marx to Friedman: The Russian Way?

The Soviet Academy's celebrated journal *Voprosi Ekonomiki* (*Problems of Economics*) published an especially laudatory commentary on Milton Friedman in 1989. The author of the article was none other than the journal's editor, who became even more famous later when he was mayor of Moscow for a time: Gavril Popov. He wrote that the Chicago School had drawn attention to "the unquestionable limits to centralized management of human society and the contradictions, dangers, and dead-end streets of centralism in both social systems—capitalist and socialist."

> The conception of stabilization of the American economy and the famous "Reaganomics," that enabled the United States to overcome serious difficulties, to weaken inflation, and strengthen the dollar, became a triumph of Friedman's theories. After Keynesianism, the conceptions of the "Chicago School" became the second example of the direct—and effective—invasion of the real U.S. economy by economic theory.
>
> Beyond a doubt, many years of discussions between Keynesians and the "Chicago School" have a direct bearing on many problems of our *perestroika* and the measures that are being proposed today to solve these problems. In the foreword to *Capital*, K. Marx said to the German reader concerning the English foundation of his theoretical conclusions: "Is this not your history?" And added: "A country that is industrially more developed shows the less developed country only the picture of its own future."

Source: Gavril Popov, "The Rebellion Against Keynesianism: Milton Friedman," *Voprosi Ekonomiki,* no. 12 (1989), trans. in *Problems of Economics* 33, no. 5 (Sept. 1990): 100 and 102–103.

that the lack of clearly defined owners was the cause of the fundamental irrationality in socialism.

The 1980s saw a wave of economic liberalism in the West with the accession of Margaret Thatcher and Ronald Reagan to power, followed by the widespread infatuation with the theses of the Chicago School and the return to favor of the Austrian tradition (von Mises, Hayek). After a while, this wave would reach the East with a popularity that was unexpected but that does make a certain amount of sense if put in the context of the political and economic situation discussed previously.

The impact of monetarism also came from the IMF, which was negotiating with the most highly indebted countries during this period: Poland and Hungary. The negotiations with the IMF brought many economists into contact with the policy of structural adjustment, which it had been supporting. The well-documented reports on these economies (including China) by the World Bank had some influence among their policymakers. The 1989 radical stabilization plan adopted in Poland was issued under Balcerowicz's name, but it was developed with the help of the IMF's experts and the World Bank's star economist, Jeffrey Sachs, of Harvard, a specialist on Latin American affairs. This program was also the inspiration for Shatalin and Yavlinsky's well-known "500-days plan" in the Soviet Union, stillborn in 1990.

The Twilight of Market Socialism

The radical reformers of the 1960s wanted to combine state ownership and a regulated market, which one could call a model of *market socialism*. This notion was different from the one advanced by Oskar Lange in the course of his famous polemic during the 1930s with the economists of the Vienna School, Ludwig von Mises and Friedrich von Hayek. Lange had defended the idea that socialism (as based on state ownership) could achieve the liberal ideal of a general equilibrium more easily than capitalism because central planners would be able to discover the structure of equilibrium prices through a process of "trial and error" such as the one put forth by Walras. For the Austrian economists, however, the market is not a mechanism for reaching equilibrium but a procedure of information processing, one based on and requiring private ownership. This academic debate affected the reformers only indirectly (through the Polish economists in the 1950s). Nonetheless, a common assumption connected Lange's model from the interwar years with those of the radical reformers: the idea that with an adequate institutional framework and correct incentives state enterprise managers would behave in the same way as those of private firms in a capitalist market economy.

The Liberal Oscillation

In the foreword to his 1990 work, *The Road to a Free Economy,* whose title drew on Hayek's 1944 book, *The Road to Serfdom,* Janos Kornaï wrote:

This book does not represent a philosophy and ethical outlook shared by everyone in Eastern Europe. The title points out its central idea, which is *freedom.* It is the approach of *liberal* thought (using the term "liberal" in accordance with its European tradition). Respect for autonomy and self-determination, for the rights of the individual, is its focus. By contrast, it advocates a narrowed scope for state activities. ... Perhaps the role of government will be reconsidered at a later stage. But right now, in the beginning of the transformation process, people are really fed up with the excesses of state intervention, with the totalitarian power of the bureaucracy. It is probably inevitable that history moves not in a straight line, but like a pendulum. Following a number of decades in which a maximal state prevailed, it is now time to take great steps in the direction of a minimal state. Perhaps later generations will be able to envisage a more moderate midway.

Source: Janos Kornaï, *The Road to a Free Economy: Shifting from a Socialist System: The Example of Hungary* (New York: W. W. Norton, 1990), pp. 21–22.

This argument would be subjected to serious criticism in the 1980s, especially in Hungary, where Laszlo Antal, for example, would criticize the "illusion of regulation" or when Janos Kornaï would belittle it as "naïve reformism." In the second half of the 1980s, support for any form of market socialism deteriorated, a tendency magnified by disillusionment with self-management. Moreover, its remaining partisans found themselves increasingly on the defensive.

Two 1989 publications that came out before the Eastern European revolutions illustrate this turning point. The Hungarian journal *Acta Œconomica* had a special issue on market socialism. Very few of the Eastern European economists who contributed articles supported it at all. Most of the support for market socialism came from Western contributors, and they could only do so in general and theoretical terms. In *From Marx to the Market,* subtitled *Socialism in Search of an Economic System,* Wlodzimierz Brus and Kazimierz Laski called the model of planning combined with a regulated market "flawed." Acknowledging the criticism of the instrumental vision of the market, they also conceded to the Hungarians that the refusal to allow a capital market had been one of the reasons for the continuation of bureaucratic coordination. Brus and Laski thus defended a "full-fledged market socialism," which would be based on a policy of full employment while integrating a capital market. In order to achieve that, it would be necessary to allow changes in the forms of ownership, which, in any case, would be needed to stimulate Schumpeterian entrepreneurship. Market socialism thus remained a goal, but its definition grew vaguer and vaguer: It became an "open economic system."

Even after he emigrated in 1970, Brus remained an authority on reformist thought in Eastern Europe. His evolution and the relative isolation of his defense of a revitalized market socialism—much closer to Western capitalism—illustrates the growing radicalism of a large number of reformist economists in many countries.

The Illusion of Regulation

The regulation illusion ... is the idea that enterprise behavior can easily be controlled by the planners by manipulation of certain regulators (e.g. prices, taxes, loans, etc.). With the help of certain carefully designed regulators controlling wages, prices or enterprise net income, the reformers hope that it will be possible to steer the enterprises in a socially rational direction. Experience has shown that this is much more difficult than many economists have traditionally believed. Indeed, experience shows that this traditional belief of many economists is, to a considerable extent, an "illusion." The reasons for this seem to be as follows:

- The enterprises react to a whole complex of economic, social and political factors. Change in just one of the economic regulators is likely to be too weak a signal to have the desired effect.
- It is impossible to develop a completely watertight system of rules and regulations. The enterprises generally learn how to use the letter of the rules to avoid their intention. (This is analogous to how Western firms and individuals learn to use tax regulations to achieve their own objectives, rather than those of the authorities, by judicious avoidance measures.)
- The reaction of the enterprises may be different from what the designers of the regulations expected because the goals of the enterprises are other than those hoped for by the planners. For example, the planners may assume that the enterprises are profit maximizers and design their regulators accordingly. The enterprises, however, may be more interested in growth than profits.

The critique of the regulation illusion, which was developed by Hungarian economists reflecting on the experience of their country, is analogous to the rational expectations critique of the Keynesian belief in the easy controllability of the economy.

Source: Michael Ellman, *Socialist Planning,* 2d ed. (New York: Cambridge University Press, 1989), p. 81.

An Accusation Against "Naïve Reformers"

In 1986, Janos Kornaï criticized in retrospect the pioneers of reforms and their ideas, namely: himself (in his 1959 book on *Overcentralization*), Wlodzimierz Brus, Yevgeni Liberman, and Ota Sik. Their theses, he wrote, inspired the Hungarian reform of 1968, and they reappeared in the Chinese publications of the 1980s. The prescriptions of these authors were similar: autonomy of the enterprise, right price signals, profit incentive, use of market forces, shift toward a buyers' market, and so on.

> The naïve reformer does not recognize the conflicts between indirect bureaucratic control and the market. He thinks that abandoning the command system and turning from direct to indirect control is a sufficient condition for the vigourous operation of a market. ... [For him] the market is an "instrument" in the hands of the central policy maker. ...
>
> The faith placed in the harmonious, mutually correcting duality of "plan" and "market" (or, in the language of the present paper, bureaucracy and market) is the centerpiece of the pioneers' naïveté. ...
>
> The pioneer reformers wanted to reassure all members of the bureaucracy that there would be ample scope for their activity. Their intention is understandable. The reform is a movement from "above" a voluntary change of behavior on the side of the controllers and not an uprising from "below" on the side of those who are controlled. There is, therefore, a stubborn inner contradiction in the whole reform process: how to get the active participation of the very people who will lose a part of their power if the process is successful. ...
>
> The naïve reformers were concerned with the problems of the state-owned sector and did not spend much hard thought on a reconsideration of the nonstate sectors' role. It turned out, however, that up to the present time, it has been just the nonstate sectors that have brought the most tangible changes into the life of the economy. ...
>
> [Expressing his sympathy for the Hungarian "radical reformers" of the 1980s (like Reszö Nyers, Marton Tardos, Tamas Bauer, Laszlo Antal), Kornaï nevertheless added that in his view, the problem of property rights had not been fully worked out by those authors, and he concluded:] Is the traditional form of state ownership compatible with the changes proposed [by the radical reformers], including strong profit motivation, free entry, hard budget constraint, flexible wage determination, workable capital market?

Source: Janos Kornaï, "The Hungarian Reform Process: Visions, Hopes, and Reality," *Journal of Economic Literature* 24 (Dec. 1986): 1728–1733.

13 The New Yugoslav Experiments (1965–1991)

During the 1960s, the evolution of institutional change in the economy entered a new stage with Yugoslavia's systemic "mutation." The institutional base was transformed, albeit incompletely. The single party remained, but it was partially fragmented along regional lines and could no longer count on a nomenklatura to control enterprises. The system of ownership and management of capital was no longer directed by the state because of self-management at the enterprise level and the creation of "social ownership." Although Yugoslav society and economy were far from the self-managed democracy depicted by LCY ideologues, the reduction in the state's role in regulation and redistribution that went into effect in 1965 took the country further away from the Soviet model on which it was originally based. The systemic change accelerated a shift in the regulation mode and development style of the country.

Self-Managed Market Socialism

The most important aspects of the reform of 1965 with its liberal orientation were the reduction in the scale of state redistribution and the complete autonomy granted enterprises in making investment decisions. Taxation of enterprises was eased through the lowering of, and later the elimination of, all taxes deposited in the state's investment funds as well as the interest paid on loans previously issued by the state. The remaining taxes (on wages and income retained by the enterprises) now went to special extrabudgetary accounts at different levels—local, republic, and federal—that were targeted for specific expenses rather than to social investment funds, which had been used for the former redistribution system. The social investment funds, except for "funds for the accelerated growth of underdeveloped regions," were abolished.

The banking system was at the heart of the 1965 reform, with its law on banks and credit. The monobank was all but eliminated, and banks became commercial institutions authorized to extend credit without territorial restrictions. These new banks would now be established at the initiative of local authorities *and enterprises*. They were subject to oversight

The Disappearance of the Plan in the 1965 Model

[The model corresponding to the Yugoslavian system of self-management eliminated] all those limitations which we regard as inseparable from a *regulated* market mechanism in a planned economy. If the process of socialisation is to consist in the development of direct social ownership by associated producers, the area of direct allocation of resources by the state must diminish and thus what we call the basic, central-level, macro-economic decisions can be at most a relic, but not however a principle, setting the frame of operation of decentralised enterprise decision making and the functioning of the market mechanism. Similarly, it would be contrary to the basic assumptions of the self-management model to impose "rules of behavior" on enterprises from above; these rules must result in a natural way from the supreme principle of self-management of the collective. ...

Yugoslav theoretical writings frequently "dot the i" by defining the socialist economy simply as a commodity economy.

Source: Wlodzimierz Brus, *Socialist Ownership and Political Systems* (London: Routledge and Kegan Paul, 1975), pp. 75–76.

Decentralization and Regional Interests

[In the debates that preceded the reform of 1965,] there were differences of opinion about the rate at which the less developed regions should catch up with the rest of the country. Because few really believed that rapid development of the less developed regions was also a maximum growth policy for the nation, and fewer still believed that their rapid development was economically more beneficial to the already advanced areas than an equivalent amount of investment would have been, there was bound to be a conflict of interest between the backward and the developed regions. Those from the less developed regions did not believe that capital would flow to those regions on the basis of market criteria alone. It was in their own interest, thus, to advocate a continuation of investment planning that they believed would be more beneficial to them. For the same reason, it was natural that those from the developed regions wanted to see investment planning curtailed and market criteria employed to allocate resources, with a specific political decision about the volume of "aid" to the less developed regions.

Source: Deborah Milenkovich, *Plan and Market in Yugoslav Economic Thought* (New Haven: Yale University Press, 1971), pp. 185–186.

by their founders through the voting system in the management boards (with a maximum of 10 percent of the votes going to each founding organism). After 1971, the Federal National Bank, as well as eight other national banks (one each for the six republics and two autonomous provinces), became more like classical central banks.

These reforms allowed the republican and provincial banks to expand their role in financing investment, and they accounted for half the total in 1971. After 1965, the power of the banks increased and was magnified by the concentration in the sector as a whole (there were 220 banks in 1963, 64 in 1970). The firms that founded banks gained cheap and easy credit—owing to their dual role as managers and borrowers—at the expense of the enterprises that had not founded any. Along with the accommodating policies of the central bank and the extensive liberalization of price setting that went into effect in 1965, the new banking system became one of the causes of the inflationary pressures that appeared at the end of the 1960s. The annual inflation rate went from 7 percent in the period 1960–1964 to 17 percent in 1969–1974. The increase in wages, an important outgrowth of self-management, was another of the causes. In 1966 and 1967, nominal individual income went up nearly 60 percent over the two-year period.

New Reforms During the 1970s

In the early 1970s, Tito was afraid that the new liberal policies would have centrifugal tendencies, for example, as Serbs and Croats heatedly debated the costs and benefits of the reform and as macroeconomic tensions increased. A new system was gradually put into place based on constitutional amendments in 1971, a new constitution in 1974, and the law on associated labor in 1976. This system intensified the characteristics that had made Yugoslavia unique in the history of the socialist economies, but in many respects, it was a compromise between the centralizers and decentralizers. The centralizers won the reintroduction of an overall planning system (affecting in particular the distribution of income), limits on the role of the market, and an expansion of the Communist League's role as a unifying force vis-à-vis regional and local forces. Reformers could count as victories the decentralization of plan construction, the reliance on voluntary agreements and consensus, and the veto power given microeconomic agents. The two main factions shared a commitment to the continuation of self-management at the enterprise level as well as in social organizations, which were now also run using those procedures. In 1971, the self-management organizations were divided up into smaller "basic organizations of associated labor" (BOAL [OOUR is the acronym for the Serbo-Croatian term]). They were

The Sociology of Self-Management in the 1970s

The power structure was in fact oligarchical, making the director, not the council, preeminent. Rank and file workers, were in a secondary position in relation to management, technical experts, and the workers' council itself. Normally, there was limited attendance at general assembly meetings, and its members were most concerned about the impact of managerial decisions on workers' incomes.

In the councils—the majority of whose members were workers—middle-level managers, people with higher education, and white-collar workers were overrepresented (nowadays, the director and other top managers cannot be members of the council). The councils were typically composed of highly skilled workers, who sometimes saw their participation as a way of accelerating their own upward mobility. The director and the experts, on the one hand, and the council, on the other, negotiated and together made the basic decisions. The former were in a stronger position because of their technical expertise, access to information, and relationships with people and organizations outside the enterprise. Competition in the market and the political influence of the YCL reinforced the hierarchical tendencies in the OALs and to a lesser degree in the BOALs. Thus, between 1965 and 1973, the period of the most radical "liberalism" in Yugoslavia, self-management would seem to have been most beneficial to the technostructure. Today, the directors exercise a kind of hegemony because they can draw on the support of their immediate subordinates and their relationship with the League's apparatus. But the director is no autocrat. He is in a complex situation as the manager of "self-management capital" confronted with the market and competition, as an administrator named by the workers' council, and as a local politician trying not to alienate his constituents. Finally, even though it is more subtle and indirect than in Soviet-type systems, the influence of the Party is also there and is felt not only in the communes and republics but also in the enterprise.

Source: Bernard Chavance, "Trois types d'économie socialiste: Union soviétique, Yougoslavie, Chine: Pour une approche comparative," *Critiques de l'économie politique,* no. 19 (Apr.-June 1982): 51–52.

the smallest market units compatible with existing technical conditions. The firms ("organizations of associated labor," or OAL) were thus often divided into several BOALs, each with its own council. Bureaucratic formalism and organizational egoism led quickly to an inefficient "OOURization" of the economy (the Yugoslavs demonstrated an ability to come up with terms and acronyms every bit as abstruse and inelegant as those in the former Soviet Union).

The Attempt at Contractual Planning

The league's ideologues, especially Eduard Kardelj, who came up with the idea in the first place, said the new system was the true alternative to Soviet etatism and Western capitalism, because it allowed the integration of self-management and social planning.

All the grass roots–level economic units made "self-management agreements" with their suppliers and their future customers at the beginning of the planning process. Those freely negotiated agreements became binding contracts and the basis of their "plan." It was hoped that the different social interests would gradually unify through this contractual planning among self-managed units. The goal was an overall plan comprising agreements that had been negotiated at the grass-roots level and gradually worked into the framework of larger macroeconomic objectives. Those objectives had been set by political authorities at the beginning of the process through "social compacts" articulated at the local, regional, and then national levels.

The theoreticians believed that this program would enable them to reconcile both special and general interests, because the genuinely democratic and "nonstatist" planning system would integrate at various levels the independently reached decisions at the grass-roots level (made in the self-management councils) into the overall goals proposed by elected "delegates" and the political cadres of the league at all levels.

However, the system never lived up to this idealized image. To begin with, self-management at the firm level remained somewhat formal. Real power was held by the director, upper-level managers, and the Party apparatus, which also controlled the union. An extreme fragmentation of the economy occurred in which the "egoism" of the enterprise or the BOAL flourished. Nothing guaranteed, of course, that the agreements reached between the firms and the other economic and "sociopolitical" organizations corresponded with the general interest or were capable of being integrated in any sort of coherent manner. In fact, it was all but impossible to harmonize the different plans, and when that occurred, it was through compromise or informal bargaining rather than the use of clearly defined, rational economic (or political) criteria. The

The System Is Good; the Practice Is Defective

At a union congress in 1978, Tito spoke about the "insufficiencies" of recent Yugoslavian development: slight gains in productivity, excessive growth in consumption, dispersion of investment, a negative balance of trade, indebtedness, inflation.

> We must ask ourselves why virtually the same problems and weaknesses appear in our economy from one year to the next. Why is it that we clearly and precisely set annual and five-year targets and then have to say that we have only partially fulfilled them? What is wrong here?
>
> To a considerable degree, it is the failure to carry out what has been decided upon in self-management agreements and compacts. We are quite successfully building up the system, adopting legislation and plans, and negotiating compacts and agreements. Therefore the fault does not lie with any defects in the system, although it can always be improved, but rather with attempts to bypass it, non-compliance with the principles underlying the system and agreed policy, a lack of responsibility at different levels, and sometimes even a deliberate undermining of the policy we have adopted. Often people do not give a policy time to prove itself in practice but try to avoid putting it into effect or else formally adopt it but continue doing things the old way. This is how elements of anarchy and instability creep into the most sensitive area—the functioning of the system. A retreat from what has been agreed leaves the field open to liberalistic and bureaucratic tendencies, and both of them prevent planned tasks from being carried out.

Source: "Speech by Josip Broz Tito at the Eighth Congress of the Yugoslav Trade Unions Confederation," *Socialist Self-Management in Yugoslavia, 1950–1980: Documents* (Belgrade: STP, 1980), p. 438.

Table 13.1 Planning Systems in Yugoslavia

	Central Planning, 1946–1950	Planning Basic Proportions, 1954–1961	Indicative Planning, 1965–1974	Self-Management Planning, 1975 Onward
Period of plan	Short-term	Medium-term	Medium-term	Medium-term
Scope of plan	Entire economy	Macroeconomic aggregates	Macroeconomic aggregates	Entire economy
Coverage of investment by plan	Complete	Complete	Low	High
Coverage of distribution of output	Complete	None	None	High for raw materials and intermediate goods
Level of detail	Specific for all sectors	Aggregative	High aggregative	Specific for priority sectors
Extent of participation by enterprises	Low	Low	Low	High
Kind of participation by enterprises	Submission of information	Submission of information	None	Enterprise decisions within broad macroeconomic parameters set by social compacts
Implementation	Compulsory for sociopolitical communities and enterprises	Compulsory for sociopolitical communities and enterprises	Compulsory for sociopolitical communities	Compulsory for sociopolitical communities and enterprises
Means of implementation	Directives	Directives	Manipulation of parameters	Social compacts and self-management agreements; or, if abrogated, social and economic penalties
Planning within enterprises	High	High	Low	High
Planning among enterprises	Low	Low	Low	High

Note: This table, printed in an important World Bank report in 1979, describes the principles of "self-managed planning," which were quite a bit different from what actually occurred.

Source: M. Schrenk, C. Ardalan, and N. El Tatawy, *Yugoslavia: Self-Management Socialism and the Challenges of Development* (Baltimore: Johns Hopkins University Press, 1979), p. 73, table 4.1. Reprinted by permission.

Regional Autarky and Industrial Redundancies

A major gap in the system of self-management was the weak mobility of capital, which was aggravated by the fact that the republican and provincial governments planned and implemented economic development policy to a large degree. The institutional framework led to vertical integration and oligopolistic behavior in a context of regional autarky. Several republics and provinces created identical industries, which led to an overcapacity at the national level. These nationalist tendencies reinforced the fragmentation of the Yugoslav market, as can be seen in the fact that trade among the eight republics and provinces strongly declined during the 1970s to the point that it totaled only 22 percent of exchanges in 1980. The situation does not seem to have improved much since then, so that interrepublican trade remains smaller in relative terms, for instance, than that among the majority of the countries in the European Community.

Source: OECD, Yougoslavie, Etudes Economiques de l'O.C.D.E.: 1989–1990 (Paris: OECD, 1990), p. 43.

need to pass so many interdependent agreements led to a particularly long, tedious, and bureaucratic process that was made even more complicated by the juridical and institutional maze of self-management and the decentralization of the federal system. Once passed, the agreements became a source of rigidity at a time when economic conditions were changing rapidly (especially internationally). The federal plans for 1976–1980 and 1981–1985 could not be developed along the lines discussed above, and there was a clear lack of coordination between microeconomic "self-management planning" and macroeconomic planning at the regional and national levels.

The "contractual" planning experiment was a total failure in the sense that instead of either the central plan or the market it created a very complicated organization that was unwieldy and hard to understand, with minute legal provisions that were ultimately, inapplicable. Although the peculiarities of the Yugoslav situation, especially its internal tensions, contributed to this failure as well, the system's architecture and underlying premises were certainly the main reasons.

Systemic Crisis and Destabilization

The new structures introduced during the 1970s clearly had a negative impact on growth. The shift in the development style, already evident in the 1960s, with the growth of inflation and unemployment (despite a high emigration rate), accelerated in the second half of the 1970s. The growth rate slowed and foreign debt soared until the debt crisis of 1982 ($20 billion). The death of Tito in 1980 was a factor in the political crisis that would lead the country to paralysis and then disintegration by the end of the decade. Yugoslavia went through a period of serious economic turbulence. The great crisis had arrived in the form of stagflation.

During the 1980s, the inflationary pressures were sustained by several systemic conditions. Self-management led to growth in nominal wages that was too high given the situation many firms faced. At the same time, the "soft budget constraint" persisted because of the banks' lax credit policy and the extension of "interenterprise credit," which amounted to a type of forced credit if a borrower ran into business difficulties. Bankruptcies were rare. Local authorities kept troubled enterprises afloat. The central bank was really under the influence of the republics' national banks, and because of the general system of consensus-based decision making, the central bank could not pursue the more restrictive monetary policy that was frequently called for. Under republican pressures, a great deal of money was printed (a federal monopoly) during the 1980s. In general, these monetary and fiscal measures and, thus, federal economic policy were not very effective. One of the reasons for this was

The Agrokomerc Scandal

In 1987, the large (with 34 BOALs and 13,000 employees) firm, Agrokomerc, located in Bosnia and specializing in the production of processed foods, was the source of a revealing financial scandal. The combine had issued "uncovered bills of exchange" for at least 250 billion dinars, thanks to the complicity of the local bank that was a branch of the commercial bank in Sarajevo. The branch bank was under the complete control of F. Abdic, its manager. It immediately went into bankruptcy. Its "bills of exchange" had been sold to sixty-three banks in different regions, mostly in Slovenia, Croatia, and Serbia. F. Abdic, member of the Central Committee of the League of Communists in Bosnia-Herzegovina, and a member of the federal parliament, was arrested. H. Pozderac, the federal vice-president of Yugoslavia, who had grown up in that same region of Bosnia-Herzegovina, appeared to have close links with Abdic and Agrokomerc (where several members of his family were also employed). Suspected of having lent a political hand to the financial manipulation, he resigned. There is no reason to doubt that many financial and other institutions were aware of what was happening, including local authorities, league officials (many were ultimately arrested), the associated banks in Sarajevo, the national bank, as well as the auditing services of Bosnia-Herzegovina. This type of manipulation was common elsewhere as well, but Abdic had gone far too far.

> The Agrokomerc affair has undermined public confidence in almost all of the political and financial institutions of Yugoslavia. It has thrown a revealing light on the close relations between the local political establishment, the directors of major enterprises, and the banks. It has also shown that these groups of people and institutions have been involved in widespread breaches of the law.

Source: H. Lydall, *Yugoslavia in Crisis* (Oxford: Clarendon Press, 1989), pp. 168–170.

the small size of the federal budget compared to the republics' budgets. In the second half of the 1980s, federal revenues were on the order of 6 percent of the Gross Social Product, a figure far below that of all other OECD members.

The 1980s: A Critical Decade

The IMF helped develop a number of stabilization and austerity programs during the 1980s, none of which enjoyed much success. Public debate intensified, especially in the second half of the period. Following the seminal article published by Benjamin Ward in 1958, a vast literature on the self-managed firm had developed the idea that because its goal would be maximizing income per worker rather than profit, it would end up with lower production and employment than a capitalist firm subject to competitive market pressures and with higher capital intensity. In the new Yugoslav discussions, the critics of this neoclassical approach found themselves severely attacked. Several measures were introduced to limit or weaken self-management at the enterprise level. After 1983, the system of planning that used mutual agreements was eliminated.

The new positions developed by the economists and the politicians paralleled what was going on in the other Eastern European countries. The market could not be limited to production but had to be extended to capital and labor. Privatization (in this case, affecting "social ownership") was advisable. Eventually, the country should have a limited public sector, which would coexist with several other forms of ownership. Unlike Hungary, China, and even Poland after 1987, Yugoslavia gained few benefits from the interaction between reforms in the "social" sector and the extension of the official (agriculture, tourism, restaurants and other food services) or underground private sector.

In 1989, a poorly managed policy of price liberalization, devaluation, and relaxation of wage controls turned galloping inflation into hyperinflation: Going from 120 percent in 1987 and 184 percent in 1988, the rate of price increases topped 1,240 percent in 1989. In January 1990, under IMF auspices, the government applied a "shock therapy" similar to that used in Poland: freeing a large number of prices and imports, a wage freeze, very restrictive monetary and budgetary policies, convertibility of the dinar and its indexation to the Deutschmark. This plan broke the hyperinflation, but as in Poland, it had a heavy toll: sharply reduced production and increased unemployment.

In 1991, the problems associated with the dismantling of the economic system and the shift toward a market economy moved off center stage

Hyperinflation in 1989

The decision made in 1989 to authorize the free determination of wages heated up the inflationary process, and the wages-prices and prices-prices effects opened the door to hyperinflation. The increase of about 20 percent in real wages during a period of eight months ending in September 1989 was an important factor in the cost thrust. The irregular adjustments of administered prices induced a permanent ratcheting effect between price increases and inflationary expectations. A self-perpetuating process of galloping inflation began. Producers who sold goods on credit fixed their prices at levels noticeably above current costs in anticipation of losses resulting from the erosion of the real value of money at the time of actual accounts settlement. The annualized rate of price increases for consumer goods reached 13,000 percent during the fourth quarter of 1989, compared to 500 percent for the first quarter. Thus, it appeared ever more clearly that the dinar had lost two of its major functions: as a tool of savings and as a unit of account. In fact, the national currency was increasingly replaced by the Deutschmark in both household and enterprise transactions.

Source: OECD, *Yougoslavie,* Etudes Economiques de l'O.C.D.E.: 1989–1990 (Paris: OECD, 1990), p. 16.

Privatization Programs for Social Ownership

The federal government recently introduced a new series of laws in parliament in an attempt to assign ownership titles for social property. The proposed solution was to give shares to workers. All the enterprises in the social-ownership sector would have two years to turn themselves into joint-stock or incorporated companies. Their active workers and retirees would have the first option on "internal" (nonnegotiable) shares, which would be issued at a sharp discount on their nominal, or face, values. Purchases would have a ceiling of three years' wages, with payment spread out over ten years. Workers' councils would be abolished in all the "mixed" enterprises and, therefore, in those becoming joint-stock or limited-liability (incorporated) companies. The management institutions would become those we expect in this type of company (stockholders' meetings, management teams, etc.). They would also include representatives of the social capital that still existed. Public officials would help advise the enterprises in this transitional period, most notably in setting the prices for their stock offerings. In addition, the directors of enterprises still in the social or mixed sector would gain more power over hiring and firing.

Source: Micheline de Felice, "Réformes et effervescence en Yougoslavie," *Économie et humanisme,* no. 315 (Oct.-Dec. 1990): 73–74.

Table 13.2   A Huge Decline in Growth (in percentage terms)

	Average per Annum			Total
	1960–1970	*1970–1979*	*1979–1985*	*1979–1985*
Percentage changes				
Social product, 1972 prices (adjusted)	6.0	5.6	−0.9	−5.5
Personal consumption, 1972 prices	6.3	5.6	−0.5	−3.1
Personal consumption per capita, 1972 prices	5.7	4.5	−1.3	−7.7
Gross fixed investment, 1972 prices	6.7	7.1	−7.5	−37.2
Product of the social sector, 1972 prices	7.1	6.1	−1.1	−6.6
Workers in the productive social sector	2.6	4.3	2.5	16.1
Real product per worker in the social sector	4.3	1.8	−3.6	−19.5
Real net personal income per worker in the productive social sector	6.8	2.1	−4.7	−24.9
Position in final year of period				
Registered job-seekers, monthly average (000)	320	672		1040
Net foreign debt ($ billion)	4	$13^3/_4$		$18^3/_4$

Source: H. Lydall, *Yugoslavia in Crisis* (Oxford: Clarendon Press, 1989), p. 41, table 4.1. Reprinted by permission of Oxford University Press.

with the shattering of the federation and the drama of the civil war. Paradoxically, the failure of an economic system that had long appeared to be an original path between the Soviet model and Western capitalism seems even more overwhelming than the collapse of the more traditional systems in the neighboring countries of Eastern Europe.

Poland: From Solidarity to the "Big Bang" (1980–1991)

The Self-Limiting Revolution

The formation of Solidarity in 1980 was an extraordinary event in the history of the communist world and in the march toward its final demise. It can only be understood against the backdrop of the tumultuous history of postwar Poland and the gradual learning process of the workers' movement and of the various opposition groups, consisting mainly of intellectuals. The merger of the two in the 1970s, the strategy of self-limiting revolution that they followed, and the tactical brilliance of their leaders played a major role in shaping the demands of the summer of 1980 and in the victory gained in the accords negotiated at Gdansk. The recognition of an independent trade union with about ten million members by a government shaken by an unprecedented social explosion was of historic importance. The Party did keep its leading role "within the state," but the events of 1980 were the first real crack in the single-party system in Poland, as it lost its total control over all "social" organizations. It was, thus, the first time that the institutional base was breached. Moreover, the Party's and regime's legitimacy as the incarnation of working-class power was fundamentally called into question, not only in the facts as before, but also by means of the formal compromise that in a certain way endorsed the conflict between the state and civil society. The intervention by the army in December 1981 was an attempt to save the regime (and, perhaps, to avoid Soviet intervention), but it also intensified the Communist Party's legitimation crisis.

The social crisis of 1980 was unleashed by the exacerbation of economic tensions that had marked the end of the 1970s, which led to a government announcement of hefty retail price increases, the third increase in ten years. As in 1970 and 1976, there was an explosion. In the first months of its active life, Solidarity focused on the struggle to gain recognition for itself and the defense of the population's standard of living. But the worsening of economic conditions and the impotence of the

Economic Reform According to Solidarity

First thesis: We demand the introduction of democratic and self-managing reform at all levels of management, which will allow the new social and economic system to combine the plan, autonomy, and the market. The union demands reform. The reform should abolish bureaucratic privileges and make it impossible for them to reappear. Reform should encourage labor and initiative in more than just a superficial way. Reform will entail social costs; therefore, it will be necessary to protect some parts of the population, and the union will see to that.

1. We must eliminate the system in which the economy is arbitrarily controlled in an authoritarian manner, which makes any kind of rational use of resources impossible. In this system, enormous economic power is concentrated in the Party apparatus and the bureaucracy. The organization and structure of the economy serves the command system and should be dismantled. The economic administrative apparatus must be separated from political power. The dependence of enterprise managers on the ministry, the naming of important people to posts of responsibility from the party *nomenklatura* should be abolished. ...

2. We must build a new economic structure. In the organization of the economy, the basic unit will be a social enterprise, managed by a team, represented by a workers' council, and headed by a director named by the council through a competitive process, who can also be fired by it.

The social enterprise will dispose of the national wealth, which will be entrusted to it, in the interest of society and of the team itself and will apply economic calculations in its management. The state will be able to influence the behavior of the enterprise through economic regulations and instruments—prices, taxes, interest rates, foreign currency exchange rates, etc.

3. We must abolish the bureaucratic barriers that make the proper functioning of the market impossible. The central organs of economic administration should not be able to impose limits on what enterprises do or tell them who they should buy from or sell to. Enterprises should be able to act freely in the domestic market, with the one exception being those areas in which licensing is necessary. All enterprises should be free to engage in foreign trade. The union understands the importance of foreign trade, which is profitable both for the country and its workers. Consumers' associations and an antimonopoly law should make certain that firms cannot carve out privileged positions for themselves in the market. The law should protect consumers' rights. The relationship between supply and demand should determine prices. The reform process should socialize planning. The central plan should reflect the hopes of society and be freely approved. Thus, public debate on it will be indispensable. It should be possible to put forward all kinds of plans in addition to those developed at the initiative of civic or social organizations. Access to complete economic data is thus indispensable and requires social control over the Central Statistical Bureau.

Source: "Le programme de Solidarité" (adopted at the Congress of October 1981), *L'Alternative,* no. 14 (Jan.-Feb. 1982): 15–16.

government led the union leaders, in the spring of 1981, to change their approach and, from then on, to focus on constructive proposals for economic reforms and management.

This shift toward "programmatic" proposals was especially pronounced in the "Network of Large Enterprises," which included Solidarity representatives from the seventeen largest firms in the country and which would convince the majority of union members to demand self-management even though they had been reluctant to do so at the beginning.

Back to Self-Management

At the end of 1980, the government proposed a bill on self-management aimed at giving the "councils," which had been discredited after 1958, a new lease on life. For their part, factory managers turned to Solidarity locals, asking them to join the management of the firm by blending themselves into the existing councils. The idea of a genuine form of self-management gained support in a wide cross section of the independent trade union.

There were clear parallels with the Yugoslav system in this proposal. The council would be elected by all employees and have considerable influence over the enterprise's business strategy, the distribution of income, and the designation of its director. The theme of "socialization" rather than "statization" appeared together with the idea of a "social enterprise" managing national property put at its disposition through self-managing organs.

The Polish demands also made some new contributions to the debate on self-management: the direct questioning of the *nomenklatura* system, drawing an explicit distinction between the union and self-management institutions, and the idea of a local, regional, and then national articulation, which could ultimately lead to a new economic chamber in the parliament that would be charged with coordinating a "socialized" planning (that is, democratically determined) with the independent activity of the enterprises. This idea, however, was never clearly developed nor was the related one of combining "the plan, autonomy, and the market." The impossibility of combining self-management with central planning was clearly stated. Solidarity's program for the economic system as a whole was based on radical reform with hints in the direction of systemic dismantling (partial rejection of the single party, modification of the system of ownership toward "socialization"). The economic mechanism envisaged brought to mind Brus's model or the Hungarian NEM with a strong dose of self-management. The "self-managing republic" evoked in Solidarity's platform underscores the importance of

A Parliamentary Chamber of Self-Management?

During the internal debates within Solidarity, the idea of a second chamber of parliament with economic responsibilities (reminiscent of Oskar Lange's proposal for a similar body in 1956) was put forward. This proposal also had a tactical significance, since it did not directly put the leadership of the Polish United Workers Party (PUWP) in the Chamber of Deputies of the Sejm into question.

The following propositions were made by the "Network" in May 1981:

We must form a second chamber in the Sejm that will bring together democratically elected representatives of the self-managed workers' organs, consumers' federations, scientific and technical associations, environmental movements, national councils, and the unions. Above this chamber would be the Chamber of Deputies, which would represent the political interests of the country. The chamber of self-managed organizations would play an important mediating role. The Chamber of Deputies could intervene in its decisions only when they seemed to be contrary to the national interest. The Chamber of Self-Managed Organizations would thus be the genuine social owner of the means of production for the country as a whole. A separation in the Sejm between the political and the economic domains would result. Socialized management would be achieved, and the game of pressure groups pursuing individual economic interests would be eliminated. The Chamber of Self-Managed Organizations would coordinate the activities of the workers' councils at the national level. It would define the principal orientations of the national economy in a plan covering several years and outlining strategic perspectives. It would be the supreme mechanism of social control.

A similar proposal appeared in Solidarity's program adopted in October 1981, though in more general form:

22nd thesis: The organisms and structures of self-management should be represented at the highest level of state power.

1. Unions must have the right to initiate legislation.
2. We will struggle to restore power at the highest level to parliament. The new electoral system should give it a truly representative character.
3. We believe it useful to examine the necessity of creating a self-management organ at the highest level of state power. Its task would be to control the implementation of the program of economic reform and the activities of regional self-managing organisms.

Sources: "La renaissance de l'autogestion ouvrière," L'Alternative, no. 12 (Sept.-Oct. 1981): 40–41; and "Le programme de Solidarité," L'Alternative, no. 14 (Jan.-Feb. 1982): 2ff.

this social dimension in the broader demand for a democratic regime and a state based on the rule of law.

Reform Under Martial Law

Under the social pressure of 1980–1981, the communist authorities made new economic proposals that basically amounted to radical reform, planning to implement them gradually beginning in 1982. Martial law was imposed in December 1981 and created a completely new situation (the banning of Solidarity, the arrest of its leaders, the active as well as passive resistance of the population), which helps explain why the reform was only partially put into place and why the elements of compromise that were in it from the beginning got reinforced. External constraints (debt, Western sanctions) also played a significant role. Although the reform failed to reach its announced goals—reestablishing market equilibrium and increasing efficiency—its systemic impact was not negligible. With several increases in prices of consumer goods (which were controlled), the country entered an inflationary period (100 percent increase in retail prices in 1982 and between 15 percent and 25 percent a year from 1983 through 1987).

The principles constituting the "pillars" of the enterprise reform became known in Polish as the "three Ss": autonomy (abolition of central planning), self-management, and self-financing (end of discretionary redistribution and the possibility of bankruptcy). The disaggregation of goals and the allocation of supplies were to be abolished. However, some exceptions were allowed, and their number increased after 1982 to include "operational programs" for defense and external commitments (especially COMECON). "Government orders" were introduced in 1983. These were supposedly going to be limited but turned out to be quite extensive in practice. Having inspired the "state orders" of Gorbachev's reforms in 1987, these orders—like the later ones in the Soviet Union—were often sought out by the enterprises because they were, in effect, accompanied by guaranteed supplies, while shortages remained widespread.

The issue of ownership gradually made it onto the political agenda. The reforms introduced new legal entities, the "founders" of state or communal enterprises. The branch ministries or local authorities were supposed to act as representatives of "society as owner of the means of production." Equal treatment of the various sectors—state, cooperative, and private—was also proclaimed.

Despite the great external constraints of the 1980s, the reform measures, as traditional, loosened the state monopoly on foreign trade, especially with the West. The number of units authorized to engage in di-

Union and Self-Management:
Two Different Functions

In the policy debate, Karol Modzelewski insisted on the necessary independence between the union and the workers' council. The latter risked in effect succumbing to the egoism of the enterprise, whereas the union struggled in general against all forms of inequality.

> Even Solidarity should be independent of self-management. If we can manage to implement the self-management system we want, that would ensure avoiding the dangers encountered in Yugoslavia. Moreover, these social dangers are the only rational argument advanced by the official propaganda against the proposals put forth by the Network. This argument is based on the fact that these propositions implied a new social equalization in which the enterprises benefiting from better investment and having the most modern machinery will be in a strong position, with a quasi-monopoly in the market. They will be able to use these assets in order to satisfy the special interests of their own branch at the expense of individual enterprises or regions that are weaker from an economic point of view.

> Source: Jean-Yves Potel, "La revendication autogestionnaire dans la Pologne de Solidarité," Sociologie du Travail, no. 3 (1982): 273.

rect trade with foreigners grew from 245 in 1982 to 905 in 1988. Enterprises were now allowed to retain foreign currency earned through exports, and even a few hard-currency auctions were introduced. The zloty was also devalued several times, although it was still overvalued in 1988. Rules for foreign investment in joint enterprises were relaxed.

Going Further in the "Second Phase"

After a two-year slowdown of the reform process in 1985 and 1986, a new turning point was reached. In 1986 there was an amnesty and liberation of political prisoners. Tensions with Western countries were eased. Unlike Honecker in East Germany, Wojciech Jaruzelski was not hostile to Gorbachev, who had been in power since 1985. At the beginning of 1987, Solidarity, though still underground, demanded true reform that would guarantee both the right of citizens to take economic and entrepreneurial initiatives and the transition to a genuinely mixed economy (self-managed state enterprises and communal and private enterprises). In April, the government announced the beginning of a "second phase" of reform with the same goals as the first one in 1982: increased efficiency and the return to market equilibrium. Swinging the balance more toward the market than the plan, the second stage returned to a number of measures that had been anticipated in 1981 but implemented only to a limited extent, if at all. It also introduced some new ones, which reflected the change in reformist thought, even in official circles. The government's "174 Theses" envisioned a law that would treat the state, cooperative, and private sectors equally. Laws from the 1930s were put back on the books to facilitate the transformation of state enterprises into joint-stock or limited-liability companies. The creation of new enterprises by various economic actors (including private ones) was to be encouraged. The 1982 law on bankruptcy was to be implemented. State enterprises were authorized to issue and sell bonds that individuals could purchase. Banking reforms separated the central from competitive commercial banks, which until then had been its regional and local branches. The new banks could be joint-stock companies. Although called for in 1981, the abolition of branch ministries was adopted only in October 1987. A single Industry Ministry replaced them, as had already happened in Hungary.

The government's thinking was influenced and supported by the IMF and the World Bank. It sought first to reestablish a market equilibrium and then gradually to introduce other reforms. In other words, achieve stabilization first, and reform could follow. The government was constantly seeking to reestablish its legitimacy and, to that end, called for a referendum in November in which the population would vote on the

The Evolution of Enterprise Behavior:
A Rampant Dismantling

In drawing on studies conducted in Poland during the 1970s and 1980s, Janusz Beksiak proposed a typology of enterprises and their attitudes in 1988, distinguishing between two periods: before and after 1980–1982.

The Enterprise Before the Reforms

- " 'Ostensible' enterprise. This kind of economic organization is typical of the first, early phase of the traditional (i.e., non-reformed) control system in its extreme, command version."
- " 'Until further orders' enterprise. This type is characteristic of the second (post-Stalinist) phase of the traditional system, when command methods were relaxed and complemented by some non-directive ones." Some powers were delegated to lower levels but could easily be taken back. There was thus an element of organizational instability and uncertainty for the directors.
- "Pre-reform private enterprises include: family farms, handicraft workshops, small commercial shops, and 'capitalist' firms (i.e., those using hired labour). ... The activity of these pre-reform private enterprises constitutes a genuine market, though it is limited since it is local and constrained by the socialist environment."

Four "response patterns," or typical behavioral patterns, were observed in the enterprises:

- "Obedient." Routinized management, with "intuitive guessing of superiors' demands."
- " 'Comfort-seeking, quiet.' Directed mainly at its own interest (earnings) as well as at the authorities."
- " 'Comfort-seeking, fighting.' Orientation mainly according to the organizations' own interests, principally by facilitating the work of the staff. ... There is a strong reverse action directed towards superiors (bargaining, pressures, appeals against decisions taken)."
- " 'Commercial, fighting.' Main orientation is towards consumers in combination with safeguarding the interests of the enterprise. Such enterprises are poorly managed from above ... and more by local than by central authorities. ... Strong reverse activity towards superiors and contractual partners."

Reformed Enterprises

- "The managerial type of enterprise appears under the economic reform conducted by the central authorities themselves. ... They are given a substantial autonomy. ... However, these formal rights are given from the top of the hierarchy, and might be taken back at any moment." Moreover, the administration has not been reformed. In practice, this enterprise is close to the "until further orders" enterprises.
- "The second, that is the labour-managed variant, is practically non-existent. ... Labourers' self-management was to be a general solution for state-owned enterprises. ... Even in the most favourable cases, one can only speak of worker participation and not of labour-managed firms."

Other Enterprises (After the Reform)

- "Private and cooperative enterprises. In the last few years Poland has witnessed a rapid development of firms which are the closest Polish approximation to authentic enterprises. ... However, their freedom to conduct business in their own way is hampered by the environment."
- "Composite organizations," which "combine different types of ownership and organizational structure. As a good example, one can cite quickly developing joint-stock companies with state-owned and private, domestic and foreign stockholders."

It was observed that after 1982, the "fighting" style of behavior had become more common (including the use of new forms of organization or bypassing legislation on the books).

As the administration becomes more fragmented and the enterprises are less obedient, central control is generally weaker and the positions of the enterprises stronger. ... Many local authorities and banks have gained power [at the branch ministries' expense]. Market relationships between enterprises are much more developed. ... As there is high uncertainty concerning expectations of economic activity due to the crisis situation, inflation and the supposed inability of the economic system, economic calculations are done within a very short time horizon and transactions often have a speculative character.

(*continues*)

(continued)

There has been a significant development of informal and illegal activities. ... In general, it is almost impossible to separate phenomena which could be considered as belonging to the "second economy" from the rest. ... Poland has a great number of separate or partly separate local markets with different currencies. Money is not only the official zloty, but also the dollar or other foreign hard currencies and numerous scarce goods. ... There are a lot of market phenomena, but not one market mechanism. In this situation, neither central commands nor market mechanisms are able to organize and control successfully the behaviour of enterprises. ...

Managers are now more strongly oriented towards their enterprises' and their own interests (mostly financial gains), still less inclined to care for the needs and demands of their customers, but more responsive to those of the personnel in their enterprises. They are also more active and less obedient in relations with the authorities. Managers are much more involved in commercial and informal relationships with all other participants in economic life, especially with other managers.

Source: Excerpted and adapted from Janusz Beksiak, "Role and Functioning of the Enterprise in Poland," *Economic Reforms in the European Centrally Planned Economies* (New York: United Nations Economic Commission for Europe, 1989), pp. 117–122.

austerity policy (price increases) and the reforms in general. Solidarity called on people to boycott the election. Only 44 percent of the registered voters cast their ballots for the referendum. The authorities recognized their defeat, called off the price increases, and slowed down the planned reduction in administrative allocations. The embryonic political crisis intensified. The country was at an impasse.

Toward the Turning Point

During the last year of communist rule in Poland, the government lost control over the budget, the banking system, and the balance-of-payments situation. The austerity policy was met by strikes and demands for higher wages. Inflation reached 60 percent in 1988. Wages rose even faster. The zloty was devalued several times. In the spring of 1989, the historic "round table" accord opened the process that led to the first noncommunist government in Eastern Europe in September, which was headed by Tadeusz Mazowiecki and enjoyed considerable popular support. But the country was also drifting into hyperinflation. During the fall, prices went up each month between 35 and 50 percent. The "shortageflation" syndrome analyzed by the economist Grzegorz Kolodko as typical of the crisis of the 1980s was changing to "shortage-hyperinflation." It was in this context that the minister of finance, L. Balcerowicz, along with experts from the IMF and the World Bank, developed the "shock therapy" approach for 1990. The Polish situation was unique. At the same time that the political revolutions were still going on in its neighboring countries, Poland had a government with liberal economic leanings and strong popular support. That government attacked two related tasks: rapid stabilization and radical transformation of the system as a whole.

Shock Therapy

The Balcerowicz plan blended these two goals. It gradually became clear that the stabilization policy that went into effect on January 1, 1990, really was a shock treatment, whereas the transition to a market economy required longer-term changes. According to the typical IMF approach, the essential goal of stabilization was to reduce excess demand in order to check inflation. Five related policies were simultaneously introduced at the new year.

- A sharp reduction in subsidies and investment outlays, with the goal of balancing the budget.

Prices After 1982

The reform introduced three types of prices: fixed ("official"), regulated, and contractual (free).

The planners assumed that, as market equilibrium improved, contractual prices would expand; in turn, they expected that contractual prices would help achieve this market equilibrium. The expectations of the planners were dashed. Contractual prices developed according to a pessimistic scenario, which the planners could have predicted on the basis of previous experience. They contributed to price increases. Great shortages and a lack of competition allowed suppliers to impose prices, and therefore they were not forced to economise on costs. These price increases followed the enormous official price increases in 1982 aimed at achieving market equilibrium and improvement in price relativities.

Nor did regulated prices develop as the planners expected. In this case too, a tendency to inflate costs and prices asserted itself. Some argue that the progressive tax on profit, whose purpose was to siphon off huge profits, at the same time encouraged price increases. No doubt faster wage increases than those envisaged in the annual plan also contributed to price increases.

Source: Jan Adam, *Economic Reform in the Soviet Union and Eastern Europe Since the 1960s* (London: Macmillan, 1989), p. 156.

- A very restrictive credit policy, particularly by establishing much higher interest rates.

- Wage increases kept below the inflation rate through an indexing mechanism well below 100 percent and fiscal measures that discouraged growth in state enterprises wages funds (*popiwek*).

- The freeing of nine-tenths of all retail and wholesale prices; those few which were still controlled were increased sharply (energy prices were increased between 300 and 600 percent).

- Ending the state monopoly on foreign trade; turning the zloty into a convertible currency, devaluing it by nearly half, and stabilizing it at the new level; and reducing tariff rates.

Shock therapy had mixed effects in 1990, which set off a national and international debate about how it should be interpreted. On the positive side was the death blow given to hyperinflation and the clear reduction in the inflation rate (though it did still remain quite high), the disappearance of shortages, the reestablishment of confidence in the national currency, the stability of the new exchange rate, and a strong surge in exports, which helped the balance-of-payments situation. These successes on the monetary side must be contrasted with other effects that had an unanticipated impact on the national economy in 1990: a fall of 12 percent in GDP and of 25 percent in industrial production, a sharp drop in real wages (although it is difficult to make exact comparisons with the earlier periods, when shortages were widespread), and the appearance of 1.13 million unemployed when the predicted figure was only 400,000.

The debate pitted economists who thought that the plan had been too drastic and had neglected structural measures against those who believed that the negative consequences had been overestimated (for instance, by neglecting the rapid growth of the private sector) and that the policies had to be maintained long enough to have their desired effects. The latter group won the debate in the new government formed by J. Bielecki after Lech Walesa's election as president of the republic in December. In that government, L. Balcerowicz remained a critical figure and still had the IMF's support. This was the case even though Walesa's campaign had a strong populist element, connected to the widespread fear of plant closings and the skyrocketing unemployment rate.

The Passage to Capitalism: Great Leap or Transformation?

The dismantling of the traditional system in Poland has already gone through several stages and still has more to go through. It will not occur

Reforming Socialism or Switching to Capitalism?

The return of open debate after 1986 revealed important changes in public opinion:

The problem of capital markets and, thus, of the subjection of economic development and structural transformation to the rules of the market emerged at that time. Before, it was believed that these domains were reserved for the authorities and that the role of the market should be limited to short-term adjustments. A new idea now appeared. In order to put the economy back on its feet, there was no choice but to change the nature of ownership. The taboo against ownership, which was still firmly in place at the beginning of the 1970s (Gierek's WOG reforms), had been weakened when Solidarity burst onto the scene but was then strengthened again during the current period. In short, there has been a change in the nature of economic discussions since 1980–1981. It is now a question of whether we should keep a socialist economy while expanding the role of the market or whether we should drop socialism itself altogether. One could say that the debate about reform turned into a discussion about dismantling the economic system altogether and ways of returning to capitalism. The dividing line between the ideological camps blurred and could no longer be stated as simply as the power v. the opposition. Among those who advocated a return to capitalism (though no one used those words yet) were some people inside the party apparatus, although, at the same time, there were people in the opposition who wanted to keep a reformed version of socialism.

Source: Waldemar Kuczinski, "Le chemin de retour (L'évolution des opinions sur le marché et la propriété en Pologne 1956–1982)," *Revue d'Études Comparatives Est-Ouest* 21, no. 2 (1990): 30.

overnight or, in the favorite term of some liberal economists in 1990, as a "great leap" over the precipice that separates planned from market economies. If this image has any relevance to the real world at all, it is to be found in the unification of Germany, and perhaps even there, it needs to be qualified.

Even before the formation of the Mazowiecki government, some important elements of the traditional system had been weakened or eliminated: the general control hierarchy, breaking down of goals, the monobank, monopoly on foreign trade, and restrictions on the private sector. All this was part, it is true, of radical reform. But the same could also be said for the important systemic changes in the Balcerowicz stabilization plan: elimination of all central allocations, price setting, remnants of the monopoly on foreign trade, and reduction of redistribution. If one can unambiguously speak of dismantling of the system, it is without doubt because the explicit model the government—and a majority of Polish society—followed henceforth was Western-style capitalism and especially because one of the twin institutional bases of the old regime—the single party—had been destroyed.

There nevertheless remained much to be done in creating the institutional conditions in which a capitalist market economy could function—including an efficient public administration. Although different economists supported a variety of rates at which to implement the reforms, even the strongest opponents of "gradualism" came to see the importance of the time involved in making the changes. Some changes can proceed quite rapidly, such as the fiscal reform that was to take place in 1992 with a shift to a value added tax (VAT) and to a uniform, progressive income tax; actually, the latter was introduced in January 1992, whereas the former has been postponed several times. Others will require several years for training specialists, as in the banking system, or of "organic" development, as in the case of new private enterprises.

But a final reform remained before one could truly say that the old system had been dismantled and Western-style capitalism inaugurated—the creation of a capital market and privatization. The Polish government and the international organizations and Western states were strongly agreed on this front as well.

Privatization

Turning state-owned into private property has been a central goal of the postcommunist government since 1989. How best to do that was the subject of a lively debate that took into account financial and institutional constraints. The law on privatization, passed in July 1990, provided for several forms of privatization and of ownership: sale of shares,

The Round Table Compromise of April 1989

Union Pluralism

Relegalization of Solidarity, Rural Solidarity, the student union NZS, and the rehiring of Solidarity activists fired in December 1981 (about 50,000 people).

Political Reforms

A two-chamber parliament. In the Sejm, 65% of the seats reserved for the Party and its satellite organizations. For the Senate, totally free elections. A president of the republic with considerable powers, elected the first time by parliament, later through universal suffrage. Freedom of association. An independent judicial system. The opposition press was authorized.

Economic Reforms

An agreement on indexing wages at 80% of inflation. The procommunist trade union organization OPZZ, created after the imposition of martial law to replace Solidarity, demanded 100%.

The signatories endorsed the "new economic order" supported by the government: free competition, the abolition of state monopolies at the enterprise and sectoral level, development of the private sector, reinforcement of self-management, and liquidation of nonprofitable enterprises with the "recycling" of laid-off workers.

Source: Georges Mink, "Pologne," in *L'URSS et l'Europe de l'Est* (Édition 1989), *Notes et Études Documentaires,* La Documentation Française, no. 4891–4892, p. 149.

Table 14.1 Employment and Production in the Nonagricultural Private Sector in Poland

	1985	1986	1987	1988	1989	1990
% of total employment	5.3	5.6	6.2	7.0	10.1	16.0[a]
% of total industrial output	3.2	3.4	3.6	3.9	4.8	11.0[a]

[a]Estimates.

Source: Paul Hare and Irena Grosfeld, "Privatization in Hungary, Poland, and Czechoslovakia," in "The Path of Reform in Central and Eastern Europe," special issue, *European Economy*, no. 2 (1991): 137, table 6. Reproduced by permission of the Commission of the European Communities (Directorate-General for Economic and Financial Affairs) and of the publishers, the Office for Official Publications of the EC, 2 rue Mercier, L-2985 Luxembourg.

distribution of certificates or coupons, individual or communal ownership, and ownership by a firm's employees. Institutional ownership was also deemed possible.

Responsibility for "small privatization," affecting mainly retail trade and restaurants, was given to the local authorities. The "large privatization" of the state enterprises, of which there were about 8,000, began with their "commercialization." They were transformed into joint-stock companies, owned initially by the Treasury Ministry (at that stage, the employees could buy 20 percent of the shares at half price). In a second stage, which began in 1991, certificates were to be distributed to all citizens that would allow them to buy stock by granting everyone a part of the overall "privatization funds." These were going to be the new institutions that would own the shares in the privatized firms. The government, which counted on foreign businesspeople to establish these funds, hoped that the latter would behave like active owners of the enterprises in their portfolios. After a certain period, individuals could trade the shares represented by their certificate on the stock market.

This technique of "free distribution" of a part of the state's property had the stated goal of developing a "people's capitalism." But more than anything else, the authorities were seeking a rapid privatization, which would not have been possible using classical methods given the limited savings of Polish households. One found more or less the same idea in the ultraliberal policies of Czechoslovakia, which did not include privatization funds at the outset.

The future will tell us if the system of certificates is feasible or does anything at all to improve efficiency. In Poland, as elsewhere, it is probable that complete privatization—the dismemberment of the last institutional vestige of the traditional system—will take a long time, assuming that it can ever reach its goal.

Hyperinflation of 1989

Three events played a major role in the shift from inflation to hyperinflation.

First, in March 1989 households were given legal access to foreign exchange in the parallel market, turning the black market white. This supported a flight from the currency. Second, as the result of the round table talks between Solidarity and the government, formal wage indexation was adopted in April 1989. The indexation was intended to guarantee that wages would rise no less than 80 percent of the increase in retail prices over the rest of the year. In practice, the adjustments guaranteed by the indexation scheme were in many cases added to other wage increases already achieved. As a result, the measured real wage in the socialized sector in August was 45 percent higher than one year earlier. Third, the last important reform carried out by the communist government was to free most retail food prices and some agricultural input prices from controls in August 1989 and sharply reduce the level of food subsidies. These measures led to an explosion of food prices (an increase of 180 percent in August according to the official statistics) and an intensification of the wage-price–exchange rate spiral.

Source: David Lipton and Jeffrey Sachs, "Creating a Market Economy in Eastern Europe: The Case of Poland," Brookings Papers on Economic Activity (Washington: Brookings Institution, 1990), no. 1, pp. 109–110.

Table 14.2 Overall Growth, and Growth in the Private Sector in Poland (Output, Sales, Investment, and Employment)

	1989	1990
Industrial output	99.9	77.0
Private sector	122.0	108.0
Retail sales	97.3	84.0
Private sector	161.8	450.0
Investment	97.6	92.0
Private sector	102.6	97.0
Employment	99.0	97.0
Private sector	127.0	127.0

Previous year = 100.

Source: Paul Hare and Irena Grosfeld, "Privatization in Hungary, Poland, and Czechoslovakia," in "The Path of Reform in Central and Eastern Europe," special issue, *European Economy,* no. 2 (1991): 136, table 5. Reproduced by permission of the Commission of the European Communities (Directorate-General for Economic and Financial Affairs) and of the publishers, the Office for Official Publications of the EC, 2 rue Mercier, L-2985 Luxembourg.

A Criticism of the IMF

The "monetary approach to the balance of payments" used by the IMF neglected the role of credit in the economy. The theoretical framework did not take into account the interdependence of short-term goals (inflation and balance of payments) and medium-terms ones (growth).

These two factors explained in part the vicious circle into which the majority of countries that have turned to the IMF have fallen. To begin with, these countries adopted measures to achieve stabilization and reach fixed short-term goals (the government in agreement with the IMF established a level of inflation and international reserves to reach). But policies restraining credit had a negative impact not only on overall demand but—and this was missing from the IMF model—on the level of production as well. This decline in the level of production was incompatible, first, with the (medium-term) goal of economic growth and, second, it could keep the economy from reaching its short-term goals (inflation and balance of payments). The worse than expected results for inflation and currency reserves in addition to the increased social and political costs brought on by the decline in production led eventually to the gradual abandonment of the initial measures. This description applies not only to several Latin American countries during the last decade (Argentina, Brazil, etc.) but also to Yugoslavia in 1988 and what seems to be happening in Poland now.

However, even if a stabilization policy were able to attack the short-term sources of macroeconomic disequilibria, it would leave aside—almost by definition—the structural and systemic aspects of adjustment. Now, in a number of cases—most notably in Latin America and Eastern Europe—the origins of economic difficulties did not lie in the short-term problems. Thus, the question of the adequacy of stabilization policies took on great importance. Even though the IMF's approach sought to apply a short-term policy of stabilization before any structural adjustment, it seems to us that it often reversed the logic of a policy that might pull a country out of its economic difficulties. The examples of Argentina and Poland seem to confirm that a systemic framework and a structural policy have to come before any successful attempt at stabilization.

Source: Pavel Dembinski and Jacques Morisset, "Les politiques de stabilisation du F.M.I.: Une tentative d'évaluation pour l'Amérique latine et l'Europe de l'Est," *Revue d'Études Comparatives Est-Ouest* 21, no. 4 (1990): 91.

The Social "Safety Net"

In Poland, an unemployment benefit system, financed by contributions from the employers and government transfers, was introduced on the eve of the stabilization programme. Not surprisingly, the number of employment offices, which are to organize the labour exchange, is still insufficient and the creation of an efficient administration is hindered by a shortage of qualified staff. The general rule is that only persons who were employed for at least six months during the year preceding their unemployment are eligible for these benefits which, as a general rule, cannot exceed 95 per cent of the minimum wage. The expenditures and revenues related to other parts of the social security system are administered in separate funds mainly financed by employer's contributions. ...

Measures designed to encourage labour mobility and retraining, as well as the re-structuring of firms, are not only running against the financial constraints of a tight budget, but have proved inadequate because of the much larger than expected rise in unemployment. ... Labour mobility is restricted by an acute shortage of housing especially in the more industrialized regions of Poland.

Source: Economic Commission for Europe (UN), *Economic Survey of Europe in 1990–1991* (New York: United Nations, 1991), p. 149.

Public Opinion on Privatization

The Center for the Study of Public Opinion (GBOS) has carried out several surveys that show that privatization is not considered the most important problem. Nonetheless, the majority of Poles recognize that it would be good for the economy even if it meant that a number of enterprises would go bankrupt. According to the people interviewed, privatization would allow wage increases and improved job skills among workers as well as managers. Nonetheless, barely a quarter of those questioned declared their willingness to take part in this process. That reticence was motivated by a lack of funds and the total public ignorance of the way the new system would work. ... Another social problem associated with privatization is the role of the old communist *nomenklatura,* which is taking part in the development of the new private sector and eliciting strong reactions from the Polish people. The *nomenklatura* has access to substantial sources of investment capital that are vital to the success of privatization. Furthermore, its members are well entrenched in key institutions, such as those responsible for foreign trade, where they have professional experience and a good knowledge of foreign countries.

Source: Artur Borzeda, "La privatisation en Pologne," *Le Courrier des pays de l'Est,* no. 359 (Apr. 1991): 19.

Spontaneous Privatizations in Poland and Hungary

Before the major political changes this year, both Hungary and Poland witnessed a spate of "spontaneous" privatizations, where, typically, managers would imaginatively exploit loopholes in legislation designed to transform enterprises into joint-stock companies, appropriate for themselves majority shareholdings in enterprises, or else lease enterprise assets to themselves for minuscule rents. The practice was quickly ended by the new Polish government. In Hungary, there remains considerably greater tolerance for the practice, although early "scandals" led to a strengthening of the supervisory powers of the State Privatization Agency.

Source: F. Dhanji, "Hungary v. Poland: Transforming Programs: Content and Sequencing," *American Economic Review* 81, no. 2 (May 1991): 325.

15

The Hungarian Laboratory of Radicalization (1980–1991)

Under growing economic pressures from outside, the third wave of reforms began in Hungary at the end of the 1970s. In the first half of the 1980s, things changed slowly and the reform process was dominated by a new public debate over changes in the economic mechanism. The debate led, in time, to a radicalization, especially during the final years of communist rule, from 1987 until 1990. With the country under the constraint of international debt, the period as a whole was marked by various types of austerity policies, whose very imposition and implementation indicated a dramatic change in the government's economic policy.

A Critical Examination of the New Economic Mechanism

At the beginning of the 1980s, many Hungarian economists tried to assess the evolution of the economy since the introduction of the 1968 reforms. One influential faction weighed in on the side of "reforming the reform," that is, making a new attempt that would go beyond the shortcomings of the NEM. In their eyes, the sociopolitical obstacles and the antireformist freeze of the 1970s provided only a partial explanation of the hybrid and inadequate makeup of the new system.

The central theme in the analyses of these Hungarian economists is the failure of the "parametric regulation" policy through which the center was to have used indirect but uniform "economic levers" to guide the independent activity of the enterprises and keep them in line with the provisions of the macroeconomic plan. The micromanagement of individual enterprises through imperative planning did disappear after 1968. Nonetheless, far from coming under the pressures and discipline of a regulated market, enterprises found themselves anything but independent of the central economic administration after the reforms. They continued to depend primarily on their relations with the organs above them in the hierarchy. The reforms increased the leverage of the financial and banking institutions over the enterprises. The main change was

"Socialist Embourgeoisement" in Hungary

Whereas the Polish intellectuals theorized about social change in terms of conflict between civil society and the state, Hungarian dissidents developed the concept of "embourgeoisement" within state socialism. These different approaches reflected the somewhat different social situations and strategies for emancipation in the two countries at the end of the 1970s and throughout the 1980s. The sociologist Ivan Szelenyi studied the expansion of "entrepreneurial" activity outside of the state sector, focusing on the case of agriculture. Szelenyi modified the conclusions of the well-known book he had written with György Konrad in 1974, *The Road of Intellectuals to Power*.

> If the bureaucracy was less inclined to make concessions in its dealings with the intelligentsia than we anticipated, it proved to be more flexible toward private business, particularly the petty bourgeoisie. The bureaucracy in Hungary appears to have realized that its own inefficient operation could be rescued by permitting the second economy to operate and allowing the formation of a new petty bourgeoisie. The Hungarian political and economic "miracle" is the result of this policy. During the early 1980s, while real wages stagnated or declined in the government sector, the second economy began to generate incomes to maintain living standards, keeping the economy afloat and creating political stability by distracting the working class from struggles at the "point of production." The Hungarian petty bourgeois dream suggests that one can create a good life if one works hard in the second economy. One should not worry much about unions, or about what happens in the state sector and in the state job. Life begins after working hours anyway!

Source: Ivan Szelenyi, *Socialist Entrepreneurs: Embourgeoisement in Rural Hungary* (Cambridge: Polity Press, 1988), p. 217.

that bargaining between the enterprises and the central administration now was concentrated on monetary conditions of production (prices, taxes, subsidies, credit) and no longer on physical targets. According to Laszlo Antal, the "fragmentation of the regulators" had led to an unexpected outcome, "indirect centralization," which was different from both traditional centralization and decentralized regulation. According to Janos Kornaï, direct bureaucratic coordination had been replaced, not by market coordination, but by an "indirect bureaucratic coordination," in which the enterprise had "dual dependence": on the market, which without question had become more important, and also on the administration, which had become more polycentric, but still had retained a dominant influence. Dubbed "neither plan nor market" by Tamas Bauer, the system inhibited the anticipated benefits of a regulated market on microeconomic behavior, while simultaneously being an obstacle to truly parametric regulation at the macro level.

During this debate, the reformist economists developed a number of new themes: the desired transformations in state ownership, the representation of social interests and a search for institutions for reconciling them (this question clearly drew on the Polish experience with Solidarity), and the need to add political reforms to the economic ones.

A Return to Partial Reform

In 1979 and 1980, a price reform that brought about a return to the goals of 1968 went into effect. In particular, it sought to link the prices of domestically produced goods to those of foreign goods and introduce much greater flexibility in this area. In 1981, a single exchange rate was introduced for the forint, replacing the three different ones that existed at the time (official, tourist, and commercial), which made it easier for Hungary to join the IMF in 1982. Beginning in 1982, a number of policies went into effect to bolster the private sector, whose growth accelerated. By 1988, officially recognized private activity was responsible for nearly 40 percent of agricultural production, two-thirds of new housing construction, 12 percent of retail sales, nearly 30 percent of restaurants and catering, and 10 percent of the truck fleet.

At the beginning of the decade, several organizational measures were introduced. Unlike the industrial concentration in the 1970s, this time efforts were made to dismantle the trusts and break up the largest enterprises. Nonetheless, strong resistance from the enterprises slowed these developments. In 1981, the three remaining branch ministries were abolished and replaced by a single Ministry of Industry, with the goal of reducing the sectoral administration's interference in the day-to-day operations of the enterprises. The dependence of the latter on the adminis-

The "Enterprise Contract Work Associations"

Introduced in 1982, the Enterprise Contract Work Associations (ECWAs) were groups of workers who made a contract with their own enterprise for specific tasks other than their normal activities, using its machinery and supplies. In 1985, there were already 13,000 such associations representing nearly 170,000 people.

ECWAs provide management with a politically approved and entirely legal means of getting around the barriers to allocating labor efficiently in the firm created by labor shortages, wage regulations, and legally protected employee rights. While workers must stay at their assigned posts during regular work hours, they can now be shifted to more productive activities by "contract" after work. Further, if good workers cannot be rewarded within the official wage system, they can be rewarded under ECWA contracts. And since workers can earn more "on contract" than by working overtime, they are willing to cooperate and are less likely to find jobs outside the socialist sector appealing. ...

Finally, ECWAs provide workers with an autonomous organization. Legally, of course, ECWAs have purely economic functions, but they also constitute a structure workers can use to bargain directly with management in the present and resist attempts to tax or abolish them in the future. Just as peasants were able to overturn proposed taxes in the 1970s, workers may now have a legitimate vehicle to exert claims on industry. Thus it is doubly ironic that the forces most active in the reversal of the NEM in the past are likely to advance the formation of ECWAs in the present.

Source: Ellen Comisso and Paul Marer, "The Economics and Politics of Reform in Hungary," in Ellen Comisso and Laura d'Andrea Tyson, eds., *Power, Purpose, and Collective Choice: Economic Strategy in Socialist States* (Ithaca: Cornell University Press, 1986), pp. 275–276.

tration, however, did not disappear because their small number (owing to their heavy concentration) made it possible for a single ministry to maintain certain controls and also because the power of the central functional organizations was increased (Ministry of Finances, National Bank, Office of Prices).

In 1984, a Central Committee resolution on reform opened the door not only to a return to the goals of 1968 but even to the possibility of going beyond them, for example, in reforming the banking system and enforcing a clear separation between state and enterprise. Toward this end, new management methods were introduced in the majority of state enterprises in 1984 in order to develop a "sense of ownership" among the employees and weaken the influence of the administration. Enterprise councils—partly elected (at least 50 percent) and partly named by the directorate—gained the right to oversee management and to elect the director. This form of self-management, which was rapidly put in place in two-thirds of the enterprises, actually remained a formality; nevertheless, it increased somewhat the directors' autonomy in their bargaining with the administration.

Banking and Tax Reform

At the same time that the reformist goals were growing more radical in Hungary and heading toward the dismantling of its socialist system, two partial reforms were implemented in areas that had been untouched by radical reforms until then: banking and taxation.

In 1987, the monobank was formally split into a two-level system: a central bank and commercial banks. In 1985, the National Bank's monopoly on the granting of credit was eliminated. Enterprises were authorized to borrow from each other and even extend credit to individuals. The 1987 decision, however, did leave the central bank responsible for the budget, kept its control over the financial system, and its management of foreign currencies. In short, these reforms amounted to a weakening, but not a dissolution, of the monobank. After 1981, a number of new financial instruments appeared: shares, bonds, certificates of deposit, bills of exchange. The partition of the monetary system between household and enterprise transactions was in the process of being eliminated.

Until 1988, tax rules had been subject to the arbitrary decisions of the administration or government. Beginning in that year, they had to be submitted to the parliament for approval. A two-tiered value added tax—12 percent and 20 percent—was introduced to replace the variable turnover tax. This was the first of its type in a socialist country, and its

Frustration with Reform

Until the middle of the 1980s, all the reforms had been motivated by two types of dissatisfaction: *operational frustration* with the irrationalities in the way the system functioned and *frustration with the performance* in terms of economic growth and foreign trade:

> After three decades of nearly uninterrupted changes in the economic mechanism, it is little wonder that a third type of dissatisfaction was born. The economic profession and the public at large became *dissatisfied with reforms as such*. In the light of a deeper analysis it is possible to show that the changes in the economic mechanisms were often hastily initiated and then worked at counterpurpose to the overall logic of earlier reforms. It is also true that the public was sometimes misled, as when minor corrections or irrelevant actions were presented as part of the reform process. At the beginning of the 1990s there is a widespread belief that everything has already been tried to make market socialism work, but nothing has helped. This is one of the primary reasons which led the ruling political party—the legal successor of the HSWP [Hungarian Socialist Workers Party] which governed the country since 1956—to opt for the transition to a market economy system and to enshrine this view in the country's constitution. ... Article 9 of the amended constitution, which came into force on 23 October 1989, declared that "the economy of Hungary is a market economy, availing itself of the advantages of planning, where public and private ownership are equal and equally protected."

Source: Economic Survey of Europe in 1989–1990 (New York: United Nations Economic Commission for Europe, 1990), p. 249.

goal was to give a clear indication of the burden of taxation and secondly to provide a way of controlling subsidies. A second innovation that year was the imposition of a progressive income tax of 20 percent on incomes less than 64 percent of the national average in 1987 and up to 60 percent on those more than ten times the average. The goal here was to increase the government's revenue, given the growing budget deficit, as well as to limit the widening income gap between the state and private sectors.

Toward Radicalization

The years from 1987 to 1989 should be considered a historic turning point in Hungary, even prior to the regime change that occurred following the elections in the spring of 1990. In particular, it was at this time that economists conceived of the possibility of dismantling the system while the ruling Communist Party was going through its own process of reforming itself.

In 1987, a team of reformist economists, including Laszlo Antal, published a document entitled *The Turning Point and Reform,* which had a widespread intellectual and political impact. Starting with a stinging critique of the economic mechanism currently in place, it advocated a transition to an economy principally regulated by the market as the only way out of the country's crisis of "stagflation" and its foreign trade difficulties. Stressing the importance of diversifying forms of ownership, including those within the public sector, the authors emphasized the importance of the macroeconomic financial plan, with the regulation of the money supply as its principal instrument, as the chief means of overall economic management. One observes here the growing awareness of the importance of monetary issues in the systemic transition that occurred in the socialist countries in the late 1980s. But it is also an example of the growing influence of Western monetarists' views in the East. Finally, the document stressed "political preconditions" for economic reform: limiting the party's role, strengthening the elected institutions and the parliament, representation of group and individual interests, and social service policies to benefit the disadvantaged.

During the same year, the Party and later the government adopted a new "action program" that more clearly endorsed a shift toward the market. A fairly broad consensus was being built, thus, for the predominance of a market economy. Even more important, political change continued to accelerate, under Miklos Nemeth's government (November 1988–May 1990). The victims of earlier periods of repression were rehabilitated, new laws on emigration, immigration, and human rights were adopted, and diplomatic relations were opened with countries that had been taboo in the past (South Korea, South Africa, Israel, Chile, the Vati-

Self-Management, Hungarian Style

Eighty per cent of the state-owned enterprises got company councils, general assemblies or assemblies of delegates. These companies remain state property, but property rights are exercised by the latter bodies. However, the positive effects hoped for from this change failed to appear—in part because it was not a change asked for or initiated by the employees, and consequently they remained uninterested. On the other hand, during the shift the party and the unions manipulated favoured employees in such a manner that even their lukewarm enthusiasm got lost. Finally, even the few actual changes did not help to increase efficiency since they opened the way for the income-centred enforcement of employees' interests in an environment where growing costs could be passed on to consumers.

Source: Marton Tardos, "The Blueprint of Economic Reforms in Hungary," in Economic Commission for Europe, *Reforms in the European Centrally Planned Economies* (New York: United Nations, 1989), p. 38.

The Limits to Change in the Banking System

The introduction of a two-tiered banking system promised an increase in the efficiency of the financial system and, as a result, of the economy as a whole. Nonetheless, residual restrictions, the structure of the banking system, and the manner in which it functioned made it difficult to take advantage of the reforms. The way in which the new banks were created and controlled, the heavy concentration of commercial banks, the fact that the savings banks hadn't been reformed and remained separate from the banks designed to finance the industrial sector, the heavy dependence of the commercial banks on the Central Bank for refinancing, the weakness of the investment portfolios inherited by the commercial banks, the lack of competition produced by the monetary and financial markets, the prudential regulations and the high levels of seigneurage on reserves, the unfavorable macroeconomic environment, and the obstruction of the State Institute for Development against almost every plan for investment put forth by the enterprises and not in conformity with the wishes of the World Bank led to a lack of competitiveness in the financial system, especially in banking. The new system's only unquestionable success is that its introduction did not greatly disrupt the economy.

Source: Istvan Székely, "La réforme du système financier hongrois," *Économie européenne,* no. 43 (March 1990): 121.

can). The border with Austria was opened during the summer of 1989; that started the exodus of East Germans to the West, which would eventually lead to the fall of the Berlin Wall. Several constitutional changes made possible the transition to a multiparty system (several new parties organized in 1989); these changes included a ban on the Communist Party's activities in the workplace, which was approved in the first referendum in Hungarian history, in November 1989.

"Conversion" and Spontaneous Privatization

Three important laws were put on the books in 1989 that modified the status of the enterprise and the system of ownership. The law on enterprises went into effect on January 1 and permitted citizens to form both joint stock and limited liability companies. The new private enterprises could employ up to 500 people. The law on foreign investment guaranteed the interests of foreign enterprises, which were now allowed to own all or part of Hungarian firms. In January 1989, a social security fund was created to manage the various entitlement systems (family allowances, retirement pensions), and an employment fund would pay unemployment compensation. In March, a new law on strikes set procedures for regulating conflict in the workplace.

In July of the same year, a "law on conversion" authorized enterprise councils to modify the legal status of their enterprise, transforming it from state ownership into a company, and then to sell it partially or completely to anyone who wanted to buy it—Hungarian or foreign. In six months, a not inconsiderable portion—measured both in terms of quantity and quality—of the state sector came to be controlled either by foreign companies or by private individuals (sometimes the former managers of the "converted" enterprises themselves) because of this new law (or because of knowing how to get around it). The changeover came particularly rapidly in tourism and the media. To maintain some degree of order in this "spontaneous privatization," preserve the state's interests, guarantee honest business dealings, competition, and realistic prices, the State Property Agency was established in February 1990.

The Antall Government

Following the elections of March and April 1990, the first noncommunist government was formed under the leadership of Jozsef Antall, head of Democratic Forum. This right-wing party was part of a coalition with the Smallholders Party and the Christian Democrats. The Alliance of Free Democrats, which leaned toward social democracy while strongly supporting economic liberalism, found itself in the opposition, where it

Three Phases of Reformist Thought

The existing system of economic management replaces rather than organizes the market. Owing to the lack of a functioning market and competition (i.e., the inner motivation to operate profitably), the economy shows the symptoms of autarkic, *wasteful* behaviour that adjusts slowly and with difficulty. The initial idea was an incentive system which would assist the plan, and the partial utilization of market forces. Later on, we set as our main goal the establishment of a market based on the dominance of planning and organized by the plan. Now the basic question is *whether we can create a genuine socialist market economy based on the dominance of the market in the competitive sector* and *establish planning based on and harmonized with the wide-ranging regulatory impact of the market. For this we need to establish a social environment which:*

- considers entrepreneurship as a basic value,
- is oriented toward success, not toward avoiding failure,
- is able to tackle the conflicts generated by the market.

Source: Laszlo Antal, L. Bokros, I. Csillag, L. Lengyel, and G. Matolcsy, "Change and Reform," *Acta Œconomica* 38, nos. 3–4 (1987): 196–197.

Convertibility and Floating Exchange Rates

After the failure of initial moves to convertibility, the issue of liberalizing imports in Hungary (more precisely: convertible currency imports) was put aside for almost two decades. At the end of the 1980s, however, the issue recurred by default, as the question of profit repatriation became an important issue with the rise of foreign joint ventures. Hence in 1988 a gradual liberalization of imports and a relaxation of profit repatriation limitations were launched at the same time. As a result of further measures introduced in January 1991, the forint has now become almost fully convertible for the purposes of imports and profit repatriation. The National Bank of Hungary appears to be following a policy of cautious floating, allowing the forint to devalue to maintain competitiveness, but at the same time it wants to maintain the disciplinary role of the exchange rate.

Source: Economic Commission for Europe (UN), *Economic Survey of Europe in 1990–1991* (New York: United Nations, 1991), p. 162.

Table 15.1   The Growth in the Number of Enterprises: Number of Economic Production Units (at the end of year)

	1988	*1989*	*1990*
Total	10,881	15,169	29,470
Joint stock companies	116	307	646
Limited companies	451	4,485	18,317

Note: Following the 1989 "law on conversion," authorizing the transformation of state enterprises into joint stock companies and their partial or total sale, on the one hand, and the spontaneous development of new firms, on the other, the number of these enterprises doubled between 1989 and 1990.

Source: Economic Survey of Europe in 1990–1991 (New York: UN Economic Commission for Europe, 1991), p. 161, table 4.4.3.

would criticize the pace of reform, which, in its opinion, was still too slow. The low turnout at the second ballot of the legislative elections and, especially, in the local elections in the fall illustrated the government's limited popular support.

In its Program for National Renewal, the government set the establishment of a "social market economy" as its goal. Private property would predominate, and there would be social programs to protect the poor and other underprivileged groups. Various programs were proposed during 1990, which turned out to be a difficult year in which GNP dropped 5 percent and prices went up 35 percent. The sharp drop in trade with the Soviet Union and the former COMECON partners was made up for to some extent by strong growth in exports to the West. The private sector developed very quickly. There was more foreign investment in Hungary than in any of the other Eastern European countries.

There were also changes in the "regulation mode" of the economy. According to quarterly studies conducted since 1987, beginning in the second half of 1989, industrial enterprise directors worried more about finding orders than about the lack of supplies, an indicator of the transition from an economy still constrained by resources to one constrained by demand. It was also during 1989 that the labor market situation was reversed, moving from a significant labor shortage to unemployment, which tripled during 1990; in 1991, it grew from 2 percent to 7 percent of the active population.

Problems with Privatization

Even though criticized for its timidity by the liberal opposition, the Antall government gave privatization a great deal of importance, although it thought the type of policy pursued in Czechoslovakia and Poland in which individuals were to be distributed coupons was unrealistic. It was counting, instead, on the purchase of enterprises by the

The Emergence of Formal Negotiations in Industry

The legal framework for collective agreements at the enterprise and higher (branch) levels exists. It includes the formal obligation to negotiate and conclude agreements. But the infrastructure and know-how for effective negotiation do not exist. What we have now is a spontaneous combination of informal and fragmented bargaining (with the recourse to the right to strike), unilateral decisions by employers, remnants of the old system of central regulation, and new forms of intervention that regulate labor-management relations. The development of a tripartite coordination that was somewhat corporatist, including the government, employers, and representatives of the workers, completes, for the moment, the system at the national level. All sorts of workers' and employers' professional organizations are represented in the coordinating council. The wide diversity of interests is evident especially among the new and old unions, the workers' councils, and other more or less representative organizations that attempt to combine political demands with strategic goals.

Source: Jenö Koltay, "Une rhapsodie déchirante: Dimensions économiques et sociales des restructurations et des privatisations en Hongrie," *Économie et Humanisme,* no. 317 (Apr.-June 1991): 35.

Figure 15.1 The employment scissors of 1990. *Source:* G. Kardos, "Nuages sur l'emploi en Hongrie," *Le Courrier des pays de l'Est,* no. 359 (Apr. 1991): 31.

former directors, the growing capitalist class, or foreign investors. The government set a goal of privatizing 50 to 60 percent of the state sector in a period of three to five years.

After a long debate, a law on the restitution of property confiscated by the communist government to its previous owners was passed in April 1991. Two groups would be able to reclaim their property directly: the Church, if the buildings were to be used for religious purposes, and peasants, if they agreed to farm the land themselves for at least five years (maximum, fifty hectares). In all other cases, the state would distribute indemnity bonds which could later be sold or turned into shares of firms being privatized.

For the "large privatization," the government decided to follow several methods. The state would gradually sell the large enterprises on the stock market in groups of selected companies. The privatization of a first group of twenty enterprises, which were in good financial shape, was begun at the end of 1990. Others were planned, but difficulties could be

Toward a Hungarian Dualism and Corporatism?

The most important tendencies in practice have so far been the rapid extension of the private sector through its own efforts, unconnected with privatization, and the transformation of State-owned companies into partnership form (mainly joint-stock companies), with ownership dispersed among a number of State organizations. Both of these tendencies result from managerial initiative and in themselves provide no means for bringing about a fundamental restructuring of the economy, entering new markets, and modernizing the firms concerned. Thus the economy could develop into a dual structure with a small-scale, competitive private sector constructed *ab initio* alongside a transformed State sector (increasingly commercialized), which continues to be well connected with State structures and is gradually being privatized. This could form the basis for a corporatist form of economic structure.

Source: Irena Grosfeld and Paul Hare, "Privatization in Hungary, Poland, and Czechoslovakia," *European Economy* (special issue, *The Path of Reform in Central and Eastern Europe*), no. 2 (1991): 141.

The Problematical Reorganization of Public-Sector Management

While both countries [Hungary and Czechoslovakia] are eager to speed up the process of dismantling state ownership, it is accepted that it cannot be done overnight. Hence, the question arises of how to run the existing SOEs [state ownership enterprises] in the next three to four years. Analogies with state-owned western companies are certainly misleading. Running a few major companies in a long established market environment, where state ownership represents only a minor share of economic activity, is a vastly different proposition from overseeing dozens or hundreds of such companies (representing 70–80 per cent of output) in a still developing market environment. The earlier calls in both countries for economic independence and for financial discipline (or the hard budget constraint) to be imposed on state enterprises through administrative fiat have not proved successful. It is certain that legal action to transform these enterprises into shareholding companies will not be sufficient to alter this situation. So far, neither Czechoslovakia nor Hungary has come out with clear responses to this issue.

Source: Economic Commission for Europe (UN), *Economic Survey of Europe in 1990–1991* (New York: United Nations, 1991), p. 160.

expected once the government started trying to sell off less profitable firms. Furthermore, enterprises could develop their own plans for privatization with either domestic or foreign purchasers. That was the self-privatization, or so-called spontaneous, privatization route, but the State Property Agency still had to give its approval. Finally, private individuals or groups could make bids to buy state enterprises. The property agency examined each proposal and, if it found the bid acceptable, could grant preferential terms of credit.

The reopening of the Budapest Stock Exchange in June 1990 was considered the symbolic beginning of the new era into which the formerly socialist countries were entering. The symbol was even more powerful in Warsaw, where the new stock exchange (organized on the model of the one in Lyons) was located in the former headquarters of the Communist Party Central Committee. However, in Poland as in Hungary (which had already been experimenting with a bond market since 1982), the number of companies and shares traded remained very small. A genuine capital market could be developed only gradually.

The Enduring Coexistence of the Public and Private Sectors

In my opinion, we will have to reckon for the next two decades with the *dual* economy that emerged in Hungary over the past ten to twenty years, and with its two constituent parts: the state and the private sectors.

To begin with, the share of the state can be decreased only gradually, and we should strive to make it more efficient, but we should not entertain vain hopes. There is no miracle cure that will transform it into a sphere of genuine entrepreneurship. Like it or not, the state sector will retain many negative features. Therefore, we should strive to minimize these negative features through strict financial discipline and appropriate parliamentary supervision, and try to prevent the state sector from siphoning off excessive resources to the detriment of the private sector.

The operating conditions of the private sector must be liberalized in a consistent manner, and its bureaucratic constraints dismantled. Appropriate fiscal and monetary instruments are needed to promote the private sector's fast and energetic development. At the same time, however, we must have not illusions, and recognize that this will be gradual and protracted development. The proportions between the private and state sectors will shift in the former's favor continually (and one hopes as fast as possible), but there is still a lengthy period of coexistence between them ahead. This symbiosis, though replete with conflicts and frictions, will remain inescapable for a good while.

Source: Janos Kornaï, *The Road to a Free Economy: Shifting from a Socialist System: The Example of Hungary* (New York: W. W. Norton, 1990), p. 101.

16

From the GDR to the
Five New States (1990–1991)

The unification of the two Germanys, which occurred in 1990, made the former GDR a unique example of dismantling the system because of the speed and manner in which it happened. Nevertheless, the essential dimensions of the transition between two systems that the former Soviet-bloc countries went through were present in this exceptional case: institutional changes, macroeconomic problems, socioeconomic transformations, and psychological and behavioral adaptation. The German process was thus watched closely by its neighbors, not only because of the implications of a more powerful Germany for the region, but also because they were facing the same problems in their own systemic transformation, except that the other countries were not going to benefit from definite advantages like the budgetary and financial help coming from Bonn, its institutional framework that was ready to go, and its finely tuned bureaucracy.

The Road to Unification

Many factors produced the unprecedented chain of events that led to the fall of the Berlin Wall on November 9, 1989, and the monetary, social, and economic union of the Federal Republic of Germany (FRG) and the GDR on July 1, 1990. There were domestic factors inside the GDR—growing rigidity, increased economic difficulties during the 1980s, a stronger opposition, the weight of the West German model—which combined with external ones—growing isolation of the regime as a result of its own policies, Gorbachev's domestic and foreign policies, the rapid evolution of events in Poland and Hungary, and so on. The flow of emigrants and the appearance of massive demonstrations led to Erich Honecker's resignation and the symbolic opening of the wall.

In the German debate on unification, strong reservations about rapid change were expressed by a number of political groups in the GDR and by the Social Democratic Party (SPD) in the FRG, which feared very negative economic consequences in the East. The Bundesbank also had strong reservations. But the desire to speed up the process, as preached by Helmut Kohl, was given new support by the victory of the conserva-

The Treaty on Unification

May 18, 1990. The finance ministers of the two German states signed a treaty on monetary, economic, and social union between the FRG and GDR. The text called for a rapid and almost immediate transformation of East German economic institutions, beginning on July 1. The most spectacular change was the replacement of the East mark with the Deutschmark at various rates, depending on what was involved: pensions, wages, savings, or enterprise debts. The Bundesbank of the FRG would become the one organization responsible for credit policy and would take over all monetary powers. Private property and free enterprise would become the principal motor forces in the economy. Price setting was to be freed, and subsidies for industrial, agricultural, and food-processing firms were to be eliminated over a very short period of time. Finally, the GDR was to adapt all of its social and economic laws to conform with those in the West and with EC [European Community] directives in anticipation of its integration into the community.

Source: V. Lainé, "R.D.A. Chronologie," in *Bouleversements à l'Est 1989–1990, Notes et Études Documentaires,* nos. 4920–4921 (1990): 201.

The Five Shocks of 1990

East German enterprises experienced multiple shocks:

- First, there was a supply shock growing out of the new competitive environment. Products from West Germany and other countries appeared on the market and competed with those made locally.
- That was followed by a demand shock that had been seriously underestimated. Consumers and enterprises rejected Eastern products in favor of those imported from the West, which led to a collapse of the internal market.
- The third shock was psychological. Many managers and workers were disoriented. They didn't know what decisions to make. They lacked motivation. Their productivity was affected even more. Unemployment and the general uncertainty had a debilitating effect.
- The fourth shock was financial. After financial and monetary unification on July 1, the enterprises faced serious budgetary problems, since from then on they had to pay their suppliers and their workers in Deutschmarks.
- The fifth shock was external. The Eastern markets partially collapsed, which constituted the greatest threat for 1991.

Source: Ivan Samson, "L'intégration de la R.D.A. dans la R.F.A.: La violence de la monnaie," *Économie et Humanisme,* no. 317 (Apr.-June 1991): 56.

tive Alliance for Germany (48 percent of the vote) in the East German elections of March 18, 1990. The process then became irreversible, as the Soviets (and therefore all four of the victorious powers of World War II, which still had jurisdiction over Berlin) accepted the reality of German unification. All proposals for a "third way," or gradual transition, envisioned by certain democratic factions in the East, were quickly overtaken by events.

History truly did speed up in 1990. On July 1, the economic and monetary unification of the two Germanys became reality. The Deutschmark replaced the East German mark at the rate of one for one for wages and savings of under 4,000 marks and of one for two for the rest of savings and enterprise debts. The Bundesbank became the monetary authority for the entire country. Political unification followed. On October 3, the five new states in the East adopted the Basic Law, the de facto constitution in the West. In the all-German Bundestag elections held on December 2, the East Germans voted heavily for the coalition led by Helmut Kohl.

On the systemic level, an overwhelming consequence of German unification was the former GDR's all-but-instantaneous adoption of West Germany's institutional, administrative, budgetary, and legal institutions, that is, the formal infrastructure of an experienced capitalist economy.

Macroeconomic Shock

The former GDR had about one-fourth the population and one-tenth the production of the old FRG. Its productivity had been estimated at between one-third and one-half that of its neighbor. Half of its foreign trade was with the countries that used to belong to COMECON. The implicit exchange rate with Western economies was on the order of four East marks for one Deutschmark.

The decision by Chancellor Helmut Kohl to implement monetary union at the rate of one for one, which amounted to a dramatic appreciation and overvaluation of the East mark, was motivated essentially by a desire to stop the flood of people moving from the East to the West (and by the expectation of electoral support in the East). In July 1990, prices in the East were aligned with those in the West (except for rents and services, for which the liberalization was put off until 1991 and 1992). Enterprises henceforth were to pay their employees and their suppliers in Deutschmarks. Wages were nominally about one-third of what they were in the West, but they climbed rapidly during the second half of the year until they reached about one-half. The "violence" of the impact of the opening of the economy was terrible for the enterprises, for which

The Limited Initial Inflationary Impact of Unification

In contrast to Poland and Yugoslavia, inflation in the former *German Democratic Republic* had been repressed until spring 1990. The persistent excess demand was reflected in forced savings. Inflation was also concealed by enormous subsidies designed to maintain low and stable prices, and many goods that entered the official price index were not available in the shops. There was a huge pent-up demand for durable consumer goods, notably motor cars. According to the official statistics the authorities had maintained the public sector budget in broad balance, at least until 1988.

The economic and monetary union that started on 1 July completely changed the fundamental parameters of the economy. ...

This is a principle akin to the measures introduced in Poland and Yugoslavia. The introduction of the Deutschmark is tantamount to the pegging of the domestic currency to a reserve currency but in the case of east Germany the exchange rate has been irrevocably fixed.

Fears that the high conversion rate of the GDR mark for the DM would lead to a surge in the German inflation rate have not materialized. The monetary overhang was apparently not very high and the pent-up demand for western goods was absorbed by increased output in west Germany and by imports from other western countries.

Source: Economic Commission for Europe (UN), *Economic Survey of Europe in 1990–1991* (New York: United Nations, 1991), p. 141.

A Harsh Verdict on Monetary Unification

Karl-Otto Pöhl, the president of the Bundesbank, did not approve of the rapid unification of the two Germanys in 1990, preferring instead a gradual evolution of the East German currency toward convertibility. But, the "Buba" had no choice but to go along with the political demand for rapid unification, which Helmut Kohl forced on it. Nearly eight months after the "big bang," Pöhl spoke about the inter-German monetary union before the Economic Committee of the European Parliament:

"It is an example of what we should not do in Europe," as he criticized the German government for having "introduced the Deutschmark in the East practically overnight without any preparation, without the possibility of introducing corrective mechanisms, and at an inadequate rate of exchange. The effects are disastrous. This doesn't surprise me, because the results were so predictable."

Source: L. Rosenzweig, "Le discours de M. Pöhl et ses conséquences," *Le Monde,* Mar. 21, 1991.

Table 16.1   Comparing the Two Germanys in 1989

	West	East	East as a % of the West
Population (millions)	61.7	16.6	26.9
Active population (millions)	29.7	9.0	30.3
GDP (billions of Deutschmarks)	2,237.0	280.0	12.5
Labor productivity (thousands of DM per capita)	81.0	36.1	44.5
Productive capital (billions of DM)	4,314.0	1,100.0	25.5
Capital intensity (thousands of DM per capita)	156.0	122.0	78.3
Gross annual wages (thousands of DM per capita)	40.8	13.2	32.0

Source: H. Harasty and J. Le Dem, "Les conséquences macro-économiques de la réunification allemande," *Économie prospective internationale,* no. 43 (3rd quarter 1990): 93.

the conversion rate for the two currencies meant a sharp drop in their competitiveness and profitability. The recession was intense and was worsened by the domestic market's contraction following the initial shift in consumption to Western goods and the decline in trade with the east neighbors caused by the elimination of COMECON (trade between them now had to take place in hard currency). A difficult short-term crisis had been anticipated by the experts, but the intensity and duration of the downturn ended up surprising many of them. The Eastern depression, moreover, came at the same time as an initial boom in the West.

Changes in the Labor Market

There was a sharp drop in employment from July 1990 on. "Reduced-time work" (*Kurzarbeit*) occurs, for a limited period, during a difficult financial situation or the temporary restructuring of the enterprise. The majority of workers falling into this category were genuinely unemployed or soon-to-be unemployed ("reduced-time" often meant no hours of work a week). During the course of 1990, unemployment in the old GDR went from practically zero to more than 2 million people. In August 1991, there were 1 million officially counted as unemployed and another 1.4 million on reduced-time work. There were 360,000 people who had taken early retirement, and another 260,000 were in temporary public-service jobs. The unemployment compensation system of the old FRG was utilized.

The old official East German unions have been dissolved, and the West German ones have opened up shop in the East. Hoping to slow down the emigration that threatened to strip the East of the youngest and most skilled part of its work force while putting pressure on wages in the West, these unions made the equalization of wages in the East and

The Principles of the Social Union

The GDR adopted the major principles of West German labor law: freedom of association, autonomy in wage negotiations, the right to strike, codetermination, and protection against layoffs. A social service system analogous to that in the FRG was instituted, funded mostly through social insurance contributions.

- The law on employment policy (*Arbeitsforderungsgesetz*), which went into effect on July 1, put in place an unemployment compensation system that would pay laid-off workers 63 percent of their net wage (68 percent if there were children in the home) with a guarantee of at least DM 495 per month. The three million retirees' pensions were raised to a level equal to 70 percent of a person's last year's income on the job. Pensioners' purchasing power would also be guaranteed for the future through cost-of-living adjustments.
- A special effort for job training was agreed to. As in the FRG, the "dual" system of alternating between training and working proved to be effective in the GDR. Even though the general skill level was deemed satisfactory, the need for retraining existed in a number of sectors. Moreover, a new training system was needed to replace the current one, which was closely connected to the state enterprises (in the process of being privatized). Priority was being given to retraining rather than dismissals. Incentives for resorting to reduced-time work coupled with a vast job-training program have been expanded. The conditions of allocation would be subject to FRG regulation until July 1991.
- Monetary transfers from the West will be necessary to keep the pension and the new unemployment insurance funds afloat. Social insurance contributions will be withheld from wages at the same level as they are in the FRG. Nonetheless, taking account of the gap between new income and expenses and of the initial disequilibrium in the system, the FRG will have to help the GDR cover its expenses for unemployment and old age insurance.

Source: Olivier Passet, "L'Allemagne orientale," in Jean-Paul Fitoussi, ed., *À l'Est, en Europe* (Paris: Presses de la Fondation Nationale des Sciences Politiques, 1990), p. 88.

Table 16.2   The Explosion of Unemployment in 1990

	Unemployment	Reduced-Time Work	Jobs Offered
February	15,000		156,000
March	38,000		98,000
April	65,000		74,000
May	100,000		54,000
June	152,000		38,000
July	272,017	656,277	27,700
August	361,286	1,499,872	20,426
September	444,846	1,728,749	18,700
October	537,799	1,767,034	23,900
November	589,200	1,830,000	23,781
December	642,200	1,795,300	22,600

Source: François Bafoil, "Le chômage en Allemagne de l'Est," Cahiers de l'Observatoire de Berlin, ROSES-C.N.R.S., no. 5 (May 1991): 23–24.

West a major goal. That process is already under way, and some envisage its completion around the middle of the decade. It is clear, nonetheless, that the gradual closing of the wage gap in the two parts of Germany will aggravate the short-term problems industry in the East is facing if it occurs without a comparable increase in productivity. The slow pace of initial investment coming from the old West Germany, owing notably to the poor state of the East German infrastructure, did not allow compensation for the large proportion of East German capital—much larger than anticipated—that has been rendered obsolete.

Restitution and Privatization

The principle of restitution to former owners of assets nationalized by the communist regime was agreed to for mostly political reasons and has led to a particularly complicated situation in the former GDR. More than 1 million requests for restitution have been filed, including those for 12,000 former small businesses that were nationalized in 1972. In addition, local authorities have put together 16,000 requests to transfer the ownership of bakeries, movie theaters, houses and apartments, and land. The legal bureaucracy, which is not trained in or familiar with West German law, found itself completely overwhelmed with these requests. The uncertainty created regarding ownership, especially of land, initially slowed down the rate of investment from the West.

The privatization of the state sector was an essential part of the entire process of unification. In 1990, the government formed a fiduciary holding company, the *Treuhandanstalt* (or *Treuhand* for short), which was declared owner of the entire state sector (industries, land, and infrastructure) and given the task of selling it to domestic or foreign purchas-

Incomes: A Perverse Logic

According to enterprises studied by the East Berlin institute IAW, wages in the five "new" states had reached an average of 51% of what they were in the "old" ones by the beginning of 1991. But for managers or people with university degrees, the figure was about one-third, while it was 60 to 65% for blue-collar and low-level white-collar workers. The salary increases thus did not lead to an equalization between East and West, since far from being stable, these differences seem to be cumulative. In the West, real wage growth seems to be continuing on the same curve (up 7.5% in 1990) because, owing to gains in hourly productivity (up 2.9%), unit wage costs went up more slowly (up 2.6%) than prices (3.5%), which allowed firms both to seek higher profits (up 9.7%) and hire more people.

In the old GDR, in contrast, the wage increases contributed to the further deterioration of enterprise competitiveness and worsen underemployment. As in consumption behavior, the wage situation amounted to a kind of collective economic suicide. One cannot be too critical of the East Germans, however, since they have simply been responding to the logic of unification in the first place. In a single DM zone, wages in the East have to adjust to rises in the West; otherwise, the work force will simply move to the West.

Source: "Regards sur l'économie allemande," C.I.R.A.C., no. 1 (Mar. 1991), in *Problèmes économiques,* May 29, 1991, p. 18.

ers. The 8,000 industrial enterprises (more than 10,000 following the breakup of the combines), which came under the *Treuhand's* control, were all turned into joint stock companies.

The *Treuhandanstalt* has been at the heart of the change from one system to another and, not surprisingly, has already been through a number of phases and become quite controversial (one of its directors was assassinated). Control over it has passed from the hands of the old East German *nomenklatura* (quickly discredited by a scandal about the privatization of Interhotel) to those representing West German big business.

The *Treuhandanstalt* was given the task of privatizing and restructuring enterprises. An intense debate has been taking place over whether one had to restructure before privatizing. In practice, after 1991 the *Treuhandanstalt* tried simply to privatize and leave the cleaning up of the enterprises to their new owners. Initially criticized for the slow pace of privatization, the *Treuhandanstalt* did speed things up. By August 1991, more than 3,000 firms had been sold off. The "small privatization," most notably of stores and restaurants, proceeded rapidly, and a goodly number of new small and medium-sized businesses were created in trade and handicrafts.

Unlike its neighboring countries in Central Europe, the movement toward privatization in East Germany was preceded by the creation of a capital market as a result of unification, which should facilitate the process. Moreover, unified Germany does not suffer from a lack of private savings.

After having pushed back the date of recovery several times, during the summer of 1991, the German leaders were optimistic once again for 1992. Still, the question remains: On a continuum with the Mezzogiorno on one side and a newly industrialized country on the other, where will the eastern part of Germany be situated in the future?

17 Conclusion

Pressures for reforms have been a constant throughout the socialist world since the 1950s. In their repetitive and even cyclical nature, they have been the expression of several attempts to adapt the economic systems issued from the Stalinist womb and have been affected by internal and external tensions that erupted in the course of their development. Without touching the institutional base formed by state ownership and the single party, they led to the exploration of several variations in central planning or in elements beyond the systemic core (agriculture, foreign trade, private sector, enterprise organization). The reformist learning process was more or less intense depending on the country and the degree of autonomy allowed for nonorthodox economic thought. Everywhere, however, it gradually brought to light the rigidity of the traditional model and the inertia of the agents' behavior and the development style associated with it. The systemic nature of the obstacles to intensified growth was underlined with ever greater precision and clarity. Nonetheless, until the great crisis of the 1980s, even the radical reformers remained confident about their ability to improve the way socialist systems worked and, more generally, about their ultimate superiority over Western capitalism. Pessimism about the system as a whole, which spilled over into support for conversion to a capitalist economy, came quite late in Eastern Europe.

The Three Moments of Change

The first systemic adjustments in the 1950s and 1960s were tried in a context of relatively high rates of growth and in which the contrasting visions of socialism and capitalism were still defined by a deep polarization based on patterns of ownership. These adjustments were seen as "perfecting" or internal reorganizations of the classical structure, though they did sometimes lead to significant changes, as we saw in the East German case. The underlying principle was that improvement in centralized management could be achieved by enlarging the decision-making autonomy of enterprises as lower-level units in the hierarchy of control. The search for better success indicators in planned management was accompanied by a reflection on incentive mechanisms for economic agents in general. However, even in the cases where reformist efforts were carried out over several years, the economic adjustments failed to qualitatively modify behavior or regulation and the period was marked by tensions in terms of shortages, often of a cyclical character.

The radical reforms, in contrast, were aimed at forging significant changes, not in the institutional base, which could be modified only on the margins, but primarily in the way planning was carried out. The underlying analysis of systemic interrelations to be modified was deeper here, but optimism still prevailed. The sharp distinction between capitalism and socialism was softened somewhat, and there was even a sense that the two systems were converging to some degree as far as coordination mechanisms were concerned. At least in theory, there was an attempt to separate the market from capitalism in order to give it some legitimacy as a means of microeconomic adjustment in a socialist model, which should, however, remain regulated by the macroeconomic orientations of the plan.

The radical reforms that were not brutally interrupted, such as those in Czechoslovakia, led to significant systemic change, a departure from the traditional model, and the emergence of what might be called a "reformed socialist economy." Two different paths can be distinguished. The first is Hungary's. The modified system of the 1970s was recentralized somewhat, though not enough to return the country to the status quo ante. That recentralized system proved unable to make rapid enough adjustments to internal pressures and external shocks in the 1980s, which led to the dismantling of the system, well under way by 1990. Yugoslavia or China illustrates a second path. In these countries, radical reforms had cumulative effects that destabilized the system, contributing in the Yugoslav case to a shift to a form of dismantling and in China to a grave political crisis.

The economic systems that underwent radical reform still kept some of the characteristics of the traditional ones, especially in the behavior of economic agents and in the development mode. Changes did occur, nonetheless, in these areas. Extensive accumulation and regulation through shortages were reduced, and autarkic tendencies were modified. Even more, certain trends that had been missing in the traditional regulation mode appeared: open inflation and even unemployment (as in Yugoslavia and later in China). A mixed mode of regulation seemed to be emerging, but tendencies toward macroeconomic destabilization sooner or later accompanied this process.

The effects of radical reform showed that, despite conventional wisdom, socialist systems could in principle be reformed. In Eastern Europe and the Soviet Union, however, socialist economies, reformed or not, proved unable to produce the institutional and structural adjustments made necessary by the stagflation-cum-shortages of the 1980s, that special kind of big crisis typical of Soviet-style systems.

It was then that reformist thought began its about-face. The belief that socialism had failed took hold, and the conversion to the market economy in its strictest sense then came at a surprising rate. It actually marked the return to the "contrasting model" and the primacy of ownership as the criterion to use in distinguishing between the two competing systems. But now the roles were reversed: Systemic pessimism prevailed toward socialism and optimism, toward capitalism. Capitalism and the "market economy" were seen as one and the same thing, as the normal and rational model, and, thus, as the essential goal for a postsocialist economy at the same time that democratic political regimes would be put in place. The dismantling of socialism was thus to open the door to a "market democracy" as a guarantee of a rediscovered prosperity and modernity.

The Ideological Pendulum

Today's capitalist utopianism displays a curious symmetry with the socialist utopianism of the early communist regimes. The simplistic and naïve thought that underlies it often rests on a distorted image of the nature and history of the advanced Western economies. They were not created by a well-oiled machine of a self-regulating market, nor are they ruled today by any sort of providential invisible hand. Despite all their differences, the Western capitalist systems all possess interwoven and complex coordinating mechanisms so that the various markets are undergirded and framed by multiple institutions, organizations, and conventions (all of which are in a process of evolution). The state, in the broadest sense of the term, plays an active role in all these systems. That role varies from country to country but is a central part of public regulation, economic policy, and social protection everywhere. The organization of ownership, even if the dominance of the public sector has been ruled out everywhere, is complicated and varies from country to country as well as over time, especially regarding the relationship between the owners and managers of capital.

The systemic critique of socialism is justified historically as well as morally. But contrary to the false symmetry that the ideological pendulum of history suggests, such critique does not legitimately lead to the extreme forms of economic liberalism that seem to be flourishing in socialism's ashes.

The Stakes of the Transition

Without a doubt, the realistic choice for a complex and advanced economy is located among the various existing or possible capitalist models and not between capitalism and any competing system. The liberal approach, however, is doubly unrealistic. It underestimates the diversity of these capitalist models in its unidimensional vision of the "market economy" based solely on one self-regulating mechanism. It thus tends to obscure the alternatives, the choices, and also the dilemmas typical of a transition from one system to another. Because of the unrealistic model the liberals are aiming at, they also often neglect the weight of history and the special problems that the "construction of capitalism" poses in postsocialist societies. This last point is well illustrated in the case of the privatization of state property, often seen as a panacea that will replace an inefficient and paternalistic bureaucracy with owners who will actively control managers in order to maximize profits and therefore, it is believed, lead to efficiency. But it is simply impossible to privatize quickly and efficiently a state sector that makes up more than three-quarters of all industry. There are a number of different but related reasons (lack of profit motive, initial shortage of savings, low levels of likely profits in a number of sectors, and so on) for that. It will thus be essential—and more realistic—to focus attention on transforming management methods, finance, and so on, in a public sector that will inevitably remain large for years to come rather than only concentrating on privatization techniques that, it is believed, would permit the most rapid end to state control possible.

The dangers of this new postsocialist liberalism are evident in a number of areas: suspicion of any protectionism, attempts to make currencies convertible very quickly, and refusal to try any industrial restructuring plan deemed too interventionist. But the most worrisome of all is the neglect of social problems. The people of the formerly socialist countries have been enduring great difficulties for the past forty years and especially in the past decade. The social costs of the transition are going to be heavy, and it would be an illusion to rely only on the market in this regard. What is more, the stability and legitimacy of the transition could be threatened by unsolvable social tensions in the medium term. Building the infrastructure of a capitalist market economy, which was already well under way in Poland or Hungary by the end of the 1980s, will require a more active attempt to reach social compromises that would allow a smooth and positive systemic transition.

The Nature of the Failure

What lessons should we draw from these experiments in economic reform? The socialist systems did demonstrate that they were viable and to a certain extent reformable. Their historic failure occurred ultimately because they were unable to overcome a major crisis—unlike "classical" capitalism, which, until now, has been able to overcome its own crises, not without convulsions, to be sure. One of the fundamental causes of this failure to adapt lies in these systems' rigidity and the way institutional and organizational innovations "from below" were blocked by the political regime and structure of ownership. The interweaving institutional base explains why once the demands for political change had radicalized to the point of challenging the single party, they inexorably led to the brutal result of dismantling the system. As "reforms from above," systemic adjustments and radical reforms left the existing political system intact. That placed a fundamental limit on change and consequently on the possibility of a genuinely positive evolution.

The opposition between capitalist and socialist systems (in reality, the Soviet model) has structured the political and intellectual life of a major part of the twentieth century. Today, history is shifting and further reflection on what economic system to pursue will be limited to the various forms of "traditional" capitalism. The domain remains, however, quite vast, and the comparative lessons that can be drawn from the study of traditional systems, reformed or in their postsocialist "mutations," will certainly have a long-lasting impact on economic and social thought of the new epoch that is opening for Europe and the world.

Epilogue

Two years have passed since the French edition of this book was written. Since then, the countries covered in this book have undergone dramatic changes. Geopolitically, Yugoslavia exploded, and part of the country has been ravaged by war. The Soviet Union collapsed, fragmenting into fifteen states, including the still-vast Russia. Czechoslovakia split—peacefully—in two.

Economically, the situation varies considerably from country to country. Absorbing the former GDR into the reunified Germany has turned out to be an economic catastrophe for the former. The severity of the problems has been mitigated somewhat by the way reunification occurred (see Chapter 16). Nonetheless, reunification has had repercussions in the powerful western part of Germany, and they, in turn, have shaken the European Community and its process of unification.

Whereas China is again experiencing accelerated, even overheated, growth, especially in the open zones on the southern coast, in contrast, most Eastern European countries that dismantled their socialist systems face two major and often unanticipated difficulties. First is a grave economic crisis or postsocialist "great depression." The second is a kind of systemic inertia evident in the difficulty, duration, and complexity of making institutional changes.

These two great problems have rapidly turned the initial optimism about the "transition to a market economy" into a feeling of disappointment, bitterness, and uncertainty, which is reflected in public opinion in all these countries (with the single exception, for the moment, of the Czech Republic). In many cases, too, social, ethnic, and political tensions have aggravated these grave economic difficulties.

The Postsocialist Great Depression

The term *great depression* makes more sense than the frequently used euphemism *recession* in describing the evolution of these countries. With respect to both impact and duration, it is worse than the depression of the 1930s was in these countries. Despite some differences in intensity or timing, one can see the same general pattern in all the Eastern and Central European countries. Overall production has dropped dramatically (on average, by about one-third in three years), and industrial production and investment have fallen even more (on the order of 40

Table E.1 Economic Indicators, Eastern Europe, 1989–1992 (annual percentage change)

		NMP or GDP[a]	Industrial Production	Gross Investment[b]	Retail Sales	Inflation (Consumer Prices)[c]	Unemployment (% Labor Force)
Albania	1989	11.7	5	10.9	—	—	—
	1990	−13.1	−7.6	−14.8	—	—	—
	1991	−30	−42.5	—	—	104.1[d]	—
	1992	−(8/10)	—	—	—	249.1	—
Bulgaria	1989	−0.3	2.2	—	0.8	6.2	—
	1990	−17.5	−12.6	−18.5	−8.7	20.0	1.7
	1991	−25.7	−23.3	−48.6	−50.4	338.5	11.5
	1992	−22[e]	−22	—	−32.2	79.3	15.9
Czechoslovakia[f]	1989	1.4	1.7	1.6	2.3	1.4	—
	1990	−1.4	−3.5	6.1	1.3	10.0	1.0
	1991	−15.9	−4.4	−27.2	−39.2	57.9	6.6
	1992	−(7/8)	−10.6	—	9.6[g]	10.4[g]	5.1
Hungary[f]	1989	0.4	−2.5	7.0	−0.2	17.0	0.3
	1990	−3.3	−4.5	−8.1	−7.6	28.9	1.7
	1991	−11.9	−19.1	−11.6	−9.9	35.0	7.4
	1992	−(4/6)	−9.8	−8	−5.6	23.0	12.3
Poland[f]	1989	−0.2	−0.5	−2.4	−2.7	244.1	0.1
	1990	−11.6	−24.2	−10.1	−17.4	584.7	6.1
	1991	−7.6	−11.9	−4.1	3.7	70.3	11.8
	1992	+(0.5/2)	4.2	—	—	43	13.6
Romania[f]	1989	−5.8	−2.1	−1.6	−1.3	0.9	—
	1990	−7.4	−17.8	−38.3	7.3	5.7	—
	1991	−13.7	−19.6	−28.8	−27.7	165.5	3.0
	1992	−15.4	−22.1	−19.8	−17.5	210.4	8.4

Eastern Europe (including Yugoslavia and the former Yugoslavia)					
1989	−1.4	−0.5	−1.5[h]	—	—
1990	−9.9	−15.2	−13.7[h]	—	—
1991	−14.4	−19.6	−22.7[h]	—	—
1992	−10	−11.8	—	—	—
Soviet Union (later the CIS)					
1989	2.5	1.7	4.7[i]	8.4	3.2
1990	−4.0	−1.2	0.6[i]	10.5	7.3
1991	−10.1	−7.8	−11.7[i]	−7.1	89.1
1992	−18.5	−18.2	−45[i]	−36.7	852[g]
Russia					
1989	4.6	1.4	4.1	8.4	—
1990	−4.0	−0.1	0.1	10.0	—
1991	−11.0	−0.8	−15.5[i]	−7.2	91.8
1992	−20	−18.8	−45	−39.1	1,111.0

Notes: Figures in parentheses are estimates.

[a] NMP = Net material product (produced) unless otherwise noted.

[b] Investment in state enterprises and organizations.

[c] Underlined: The year prices were freed.

[d] From one December to the next.

[e] Sales of material goods, excluding agriculture and the private sector.

[f] Gross domestic product.

[g] From January to September.

[h] Not including Albania.

[i] Only the state and cooperative sectors.

Sources: Economic Commission for Europe (United Nations): *Economic Survey of Europe in 1991–1992* (New York: 1992); *Economic Survey of Europe in 1992–1993* (New York: 1993).

percent or more). Foreign trade has declined, the standard of living and consumption have deteriorated, inflation has remained high even after prices were freed, and unemployment has increased significantly, going from practically none to more than 10 percent in a year or two.

In 1994, Hungary, Poland, and the Czech Republic may emerge from this period of decline. Economic conditions should at least level off, and there may even be some weak growth. However, production and the standard of living will all but certainly continue to decline in Romania, Bulgaria, Albania, Russia, and many of the other former Soviet republics. The depression that has accompanied the postsocialist transition is, alas, a unique phenomenon in economic history during peacetime.

If one focuses on the "stylized facts," one can see some parallels with the symptoms from the 1930s. There is also a single important difference—the inflation that accompanies the depression today. Moreover, the dynamics and the institutional context are different.

The experiences of two of the countries have been different from the rest in Eastern Europe. In the former GDR, the standard of living has not deteriorated so much as elsewhere (with the one-to-one conversion amounting to an "overvaluation" of the East German mark, Eastern wages gradually catching up with those in the West, and massive budgetary transfers from the West to the East for social insurance programs), and the inflation rate has remained low. But industrial production declined and unemployment increased more than elsewhere. In 1992 and 1993, shortages were eased in Russia with the freeing of prices under the Gaïdar plan (though they did not disappear). Unemployment remains relatively low, but the country suffers from mega-inflation. Production and real incomes have shrunk dramatically. The country is in a crisis marked by shortages and inflation, the "shortageflation" syndrome, characteristic of the degeneration of the traditional system, to which is added the drift toward the economic fragmentation of the country.

The statistics available to us, of course, are not wholly reliable. The unemployment measures are no more than approximations that cannot be readily compared from country to country. Little reliable data exist for the new private sector because of the widespread practice of tax evasion. The same is obviously the case for the new underground economy. The real depression is thus probably less severe than the statistical indicators suggest. Nonetheless, it is important to emphasize that these modifications do not alter the basic picture, which is confirmed by the vast majority of the data, partial, local, and regional studies, and by the analysis of the dynamics of the depression itself.

As far as errors in the initial estimates are concerned, it goes without saying that it is impossible to make precise projections whenever a systemic transformation is occurring, and unexpected developments are, if one can use the term, probable. Moreover, a recession linked to the transition was inevitable as a result of the rapid dismantling of the former management and coordination system, not to mention the impact of the vast sectoral redeployment. The problem is that all the forecasting errors pointed in the same direction—toward an optimism that, in retrospect, seems totally excessive and even naïve. The absorption of the GDR at the time of German reunification is a perfect example of that. And as I will show further on, there were important theoretical reasons why those errors were made.

Comparing the stated macroeconomic goals of the stabilization plans with the actual results reveals a systematic pattern: Production fell more and longer, unemployment grew more rapidly, inflation was higher, and the budget deficit was larger than anticipated. Other differences were observed: an underestimation of the drop in trade between the Eastern European countries and an overestimation of foreign investment—which remained generally quite limited except in Hungary and, to a lesser, degree, the Czech Republic.

A Rapid Transition—Thanks to Shock Therapy?

Ever since the beginning of the transformation process, the political leadership in both the East and the West and the major international economic organizations have developed specific rhetoric about "the transition to a market economy," which has since come to be reflected in public opinion as well. The economists, inspired by free market ideas in the East as well as the West, have been particularly optimistic about the transition. Their implicit point of departure was a simplified model of Western capitalism: a system characterized by market coordination based on private ownership. Thus they saw the transition as a shift from an artificial and irrational order based on planning and state ownership, through universal deregulation, to a spontaneous, self-regulating, and rational order: the market economy.

The key to it all was thought to be a rapid transformation of the system of ownership, hence the importance of speedy privatization. Economists who followed this approach did not draw much distinction between the "normal" regulation in the traditional socialist economies, which was based on shortages, and the pathological forms that came into being as some of these systems disintegrated, and thus they believed that the excess of cash (or "monetary overhang") was always the major problem to resolve. The elimination of administered "false prices," after a period when the previously repressed inflation would be released (and when a very restrictive monetary policy would be needed), would soon allow a return to the equilibrium of the market. The new monetary stability would eliminate the shortage economy and open the door to restructuring and a return to growth. A rapid opening up of these economies would accelerate the process by introducing competitive stimuli from producers in other countries and allowing an influx of foreign investment, both of which would tend to produce more rational management and to balance the sectoral structure of the economy. A recession connected to this structural adjustment was to be expected, with the appearance of real unemployment due, in part, to the hidden unemployment of the old system and, in part, to frictional causes.

The transition was bound to be difficult—but only for the short term. It would without doubt be hard for certain social groups to make the behavior adjustments and accept the new hierarchy of income and power, but that was the price one had to pay in order to achieve a new level of prosperity that would actually benefit the vast majority of the society. In this approach, the change in the system would be seen as the result of "shock therapy." Above all, what mattered was the speed of change, in order to avoid falling back into some intermediary and undesirable state.

With the shock of the depression, the free market euphoria was toned down and gave way to a tremendous sense of disillusion, especially in the social groups that had strongly supported the new democratic coalitions. Therein lay a cause of the political instability and the weak legitimacy accorded the new governments in several of the former socialist countries. Even though the transition to a Western-style capitalism was never put into question, a debate developed everywhere on stabilization policy and institutional transformation. The paths and the means for producing that change were discussed in contradictory ways, putting into question the initial dogma according to which there was "only one path" to follow in the transition.

The inflexible partisans of the free market developed an a posteriori argument to take this new situation into account. According to this line of reasoning, the drop in production was overestimated because of statistical biases and poor data on the private sector. Even more, they viewed this decline as beneficial, because it revealed that restructuring was occurring and eliminating waste and the production of goods that were neither demanded nor competitive. They claimed that the reduction in the standard of living was also less severe than the statistics showed, because the comparison of purchasing power, which did not take into account the disappearance of shortages or the cost of time spent waiting in line before prices were liberalized, was biased. Unemployment was seen as partly voluntary because compensation was too generous. More generally, they argued that if these governments did not follow the current policies, instability and the economic crisis would last indefinitely. These countries absolutely had to speed up privatization, since its delay largely explained the unexpected difficulties encountered in the transition.

The Real Dynamics of the Depression

The nature of the postsocialist depression is, therefore, already quite controversial and will undoubtedly remain so for quite some time. However, it is clear that the free market approach cannot explain the complexity of the depression. Although it is true that the collapse of COMECON and the Soviet market has been a major shock for its former members and trading partners, the stabilization policies inspired by the structural adjustment plans have played a role in causing the depression, too, along with the (actually predictable) slowness of institutional and behavioral changes. The structural adjustment plans were devised for developing capitalist economies but were applied here in the very different situation of the dismantling of socialist economies.

Even though the Central European countries have had rather different experiences, one can think of a common pattern that is typical of the crisis. The contraction of demand thus had two causes. The first, and relatively unexpected, was the dislocations in trade relations among the socialist countries. The other was found in the stabilization plans (freeing prices, restrictive monetary policy, wage controls, budgetary cutbacks, currency devaluations) precisely designed to reduce excessive demand. Nonetheless, contrary to the predictions made by the governments or their advisers, supply exhibited a negative, rather than a positive, "response": It dropped even more than demand. This contributed to the rapid shift from an economy constrained by resources to one constrained by demand, which resulted in the disappearance of shortages and the emergence of unemployment—but under strongly recessionary conditions.

Certain classical aspects of a cumulative depression brought on by the weakness of demand—in other words, a quasi-Keynesian situation—appeared. Nonetheless, the institutional framework, the behavior of actors, and the connections among the macroeconomic factors made the postsocialist depression unique. Among the factors perpetuating the crisis, one should mention the following: The accumulation of interenterprise arrears or (involuntary) credit between enterprises considerably weakened the restrictive monetary policy. The general uncertainty brought on by the depression accelerated the contraction of investment, which was initiated by the reduction in budgetary expenditures and the hardening of credit, and then reduced demand even more and slowed down the needed restructuring of the economy. The drop in production led to a fall in tax payments at a time when social expenditures could not be reduced very much because of increased unemployment. This meant that budget deficits remained high, contributing to continued inflationary pressure (in the absence of a developed financial and monetary system). The fiscal crisis of the state resulting from the depression became reciprocally a cause of the latter because credit to the state tended to crowd out credit for the economy (state and private sectors).

The Behavioral Heritage

The behavior of state enterprises when the stabilization policies were introduced provides an example of inertia owing, not to the irrationality of economic actors, but to the fact that the social learning process is inherently gradual, and that process was further complicated by the heterogeneous setup of the transitional institutions. Faced with the serious degradation of their environment, marked by a combination of price increases for inputs and a drastic reduction in subsidies along with a severe restriction on credit, these often oligopolistic units of production tried to adapt in a situation in which the owner of capital (the state) remained impersonal and bankruptcies remained rare. There is nothing surprising in the fact that the reactions one observed differed from what was expected in the Western capitalist economies. Aggravating the effects of the often extremely restrictive stabilization plans, this behavioral factor constitutes one of the keys to the "negative adjustment," with its inverse response (negative and not positive) of supply, which has made such a considerable contribution to the depression.

The usual sequence was the following: Enterprises first reduced production and raised prices (in a manner consistent with the teachings of microeconomic texts about monopolies), which led to price increases above those expected when they were liberalized. Next, the enterprises stopped paying their suppliers (interenterprise arrears or "credit") or even the state (tax arrears). Then they sought to negotiate terms with the banks and to put pressure on the government. Later they introduced part-time work. Eventually, they had to lay off and then fire part of their work force. Thus, a clear delay, or time lag, could be seen between declining production and increasing unemployment in the various countries.

The Slow Pace of Institutional Change

The free market approach assumed a speedy systemic change whereby the abolition of the economic institutions and the system as a whole that had been inherited from the socialist period would permit the self-regulating order of the market to develop quickly and spontaneously. This naïve vision, which simplified the history of all functioning capitalist systems and which misunderstood the lessons of earlier economic reforms in the socialist countries, has proven false. Even though an old economic system can be dismantled quickly, the creation and stabilization of a new one take a long time. A realistic strategy for transformation should take into account that this kind of systemic change entails an evolutionary process and gradual learning (individual, organizational, social).

The behavioral inertia and the weight of the inherited institutions surprised the advocates of a free market transition but were less shocking to specialists on socialist systems or to institutional economists. More than three years after the beginning of the transition, the rate of change in many areas has been far slower than initially expected. That is the case, for example, in agriculture, banking, taxation, financial markets, and social security. The transitional economy is a very complex mix of the new and the old: institutions, actors, behaviors, norms, and conventions, marked by contradictory dynamics that have led to tremendous uncertainty.

From this perspective, the case of mass privatization is typical. As one could predict, none of the initial policies has come close to being implemented. The gradualistic Hungarian approach has led to the privatization of only a small portion of the state sector. The mass privatization anticipated in Poland has not yet occurred because there has been no political consensus for it. In fact, the principal method used has been "liquidation," which amounts to giving state enterprises away to their managers and workers through leases of five years or more—a far cry from genuine privatization. An attempt to return to mass privatization through the creation of large investment funds is now taking place.

Only one country has made serious progress in privatizing a part of the state sector—the former Czechoslovakia—where in a "first wave," low-priced vouchers were sold to individual citizens who then converted them into shares in firms being privatized. This first step is being completed in the Czech Republic in 1994. Investment funds managing individuals' vouchers were spontaneously created in the process, the most important of which were controlled by the big banks (state owned or themselves on the road to privatization). Another "wave" is planned, which means that even if the initial success is confirmed, privatization will still take several years to complete, given the complexity of the process and its management.

Similarly, Russia embarked on a program of mass privatization in 1992 when it gave each citizen vouchers worth 10,000 rubles. But the mone-

tary crisis, political tensions, and economic disorganization in that
country made the prospects for any well-organized, large privatization
program very uncertain in the medium term.

The Mixed Transitional Economy

The various methods for privatizing—conventional or unconventional
(mass privatization)—each have shortcomings. The former will take a
long time; the latter cannot resolve one key problem—finding the capital needed to restructure the productive apparatus.

In any event, observers today have to admit that contrary to initial expectations and despite the variations implied in the different procedures chosen, large-scale privatization will be a long, difficult (economically, technically, socially) process, one that will not in all likelihood go
as far as first envisaged and will have many uncertain effects at least in
the short and medium term. To this should be added the observation
that dynamism in the private sector, which does exist but varies from
country to country, remains too weak to stimulate qualitative and rapid
systemic change on its own.

Note that China is a special case in this respect. The expansion of the
private sector over the past dozen years, even though based on reforms
of its socialist system and not any sort of postsocialist transformation,
has produced considerable change. But the exception confirms the rule.
The Chinese case can be explained by the weight of agriculture and related activities and by the strong growth that accompanied the prag-
matic and gradualistic reforms introduced by those in charge in Beijing,
and spurred on by the rise of increasingly powerful regional economies.

Despite the initial proclamations against a "third way," an unexpected form of "market socialism" has dominated in Eastern Europe
and will remain in place for an undetermined period in each of these
countries. The continued dominance of a public sector that is gradually
being reduced, alongside a private sector that is gradually expanding,
has led to the crystallization of a *mixed transitional postsocialist economy*. It has a dual and asymmetrical makeup, which, though there are
rather sharp national differences, can be described in the following
manner: The public sector is at the epicenter of the crisis. It is made up
of the large, concentrated enterprises, often oligopolies or monopolies,
and for the most part, in industry. There, employment is contracting
even though bankruptcies have barely begun to occur (except in Hungary). Restructuring in these areas has been quite limited—notably because of the drop in investment. This sector is heavily in debt
("interenterprise credit" or "bad loans" from banks) and is often under-
going a gradual decapitalization. Despite its financial difficulties, it re-

mains the main source of government revenues. These enterprises still play an important role in the "social protection" of their employees, although that role is declining.

In contrast, the private sector (privatized or, more commonly, newly created enterprises) has been growing rapidly and has limited the magnitude of the depression, but it cannot compensate for the deterioration in the state sector, as can be seen in the rapidly increasing unemployment rates. In general, the enterprises are individually owned and small or, at most, medium sized. Their number (newly created ones minus bankruptcies) has increased dramatically, but that has occurred primarily in the services, retailing, and construction—but not to any considerable degree in the industrial sector (Poland being the exception here). Investment is limited, it is hard to obtain credit, and contributions to the state budget are rather low since the private sector is so adept at tax evasion, one of the most perverse effects of this dualistic mixed economy. The fiscal crisis has occurred mostly because of declining production in the state sector, but the state has had to keep tax rates for those enterprises up because the money they contribute to the government's budget could not be generated elsewhere in the economy. Even worse, the continuing privatizations might make this fiscal crisis more severe in the short term.

In this domain, as in many others, the return to a minimum rate of growth for the economy as a whole would permit the attenuation of, or even a break from, these typical vicious circles, as suggested by the opposite experience of the Chinese.

National Paths and Common Problems

The historical analysis of the reform process shows us that the socialist countries, although they faced the same set of major problems, evolved in different ways. They arrived at the great transformation under different macroeconomic, sociopolitical, and systemic conditions. The breaks with the old system all took place at the same time, but they occurred quite differently—political negotiation in Poland or Hungary, "velvet revolution" in Czechoslovakia, reaction against the coup attempt in the Soviet Union.

Along those same lines, the transformations are now to follow a number of national paths, which illustrate the role played by path-dependency in history. The way an economy is structured or changes is deeply influenced by its unique, earlier evolution, both recent and long ago. The transformation of a socialist economy is, thus, the result of complex interactions among the initial systemic and social conditions, strategic or political decisions made by the government or organized social forces, unexpected events, the behavioral adaptation of economic agents, and institutional innovations and imitations. These different paths toward change are determined by the specific facts unique to each country.

Diversified paths of change can be observed in the "stylized facts" unique to each country. There remains tremendous uncertainty about the future. Nevertheless, the term *transition* makes sense in the respect that the old system has been dismantled and has lost its overall coherence, leaving a lasting impact on the evolution of the economy and society in the process. But the new patterns that may emerge remain unclear. The transition could stall or be blocked, it could create a prolonged period of instability, or it could lead to a new system, different from the proclaimed target, and possibly undesirable.

The uncertainty about the future system is one of the common problems facing the postsocialist economies. It is linked to the other difficulties they share, despite their different paths, such as the great depression and systemic and institutional inertia. The risks are great—the long-lasting impact of the negative effects of the dualism of a mixed, transition economy, weak or unstable growth after the end of the depression, excessive de-industrialization, and questioning of the political consensus. Debate about the continuation, adjustment, or change in the policies pursued so far will certainly continue.

It seems to me that the conclusion of this book, first written two years ago, can be supported with even more confidence today. The end of the socialist regimes and the transformation of their economic and social systems already rank among the great historical experiments, the interpretation of which is a challenge, a source of controversy, and an opportunity for further development for the various social sciences, much like the industrial revolution, the crisis of the interwar period, or the changes seen in the less-developed countries over the past few decades.

Bernard Chavance
July 1993

Selected Bibliography

Adam, Jan. *Economic Reform in the Soviet Union and Eastern Europe Since the 1960s.* London: Macmillan, 1989.

Asselain, Jean-Charles. *Planning and Profits in Socialist Economies.* London: Routledge & Kegan Paul, 1984.

Bauer, Tamas. "The Hungarian Alternative to Soviet-type Planning," *Journal of Comparative Economics* 7, no. 3, 1983.

Berend, Ivan T. *The Hungarian Economic Reforms: 1953–1988.* Cambridge: Cambridge University Press, 1990.

Brus, Wlodzimierz. *The Market in a Socialist Economy.* London: Routledge & Kegan Paul, 1972.

_____. *Socialist Ownership and Political Systems.* London: Routledge & Kegan Paul, 1975.

_____. "East European Reforms: What Happened to Them?" *Soviet Studies* 31, no. 4, 1979.

_____. *Institutional Change Within a Planned Economy.* In M. Kaser, ed., *The Economic History of Eastern Europe.* Vol. 3. Oxford: Clarendon Press, 1986.

Brus, Wlodzimierz, and Kazimierz Laski. *From Marx to the Market: Socialism in Search of an Economic System.* Oxford: Clarendon Press, 1989.

Economic Commission for Europe (United Nations). *Economic Survey of Europe in ...* New York: United Nations, various years.

Ellman, Michael. *Socialist Planning.* 2nd ed. New York: Cambridge University Press, 1989.

Hewett, Ed. *Reforming the Soviet Economy.* Washington: Brookings Institution, 1988.

Kornaï, Janos. *The Road to a Free Economy: Shifting from a Socialist System: The Example of Hungary.* New York: W. W. Norton, 1990.

_____. *Vision and Reality, Market and State.* London: Harvester-Wheatsheaf, 1990.

_____. *The Socialist System: The Political Economy of Communism.* Princeton: Princeton University Press, 1992.

Lewin, Moshe. *Political Undercurrents in Soviet Economic Debates: From Bukharin to Modern Reformers.* Princeton: Princeton University Press, 1974.

Nove, Alec. *The Soviet Economic System.* 3rd ed. London: Allen and Unwin, 1986.

_____ . *Le socialisme sans Marx*. Paris: Economica, 1983; rev. ed.: *The Economics of Feasible Socialism Revisited*. London: Harper Collins, 1991.

Riskin, Carl. *China's Political Economy*. New York: Oxford University Press, 1987.

Selucky, Radoslav. *Economic Reforms in Eastern Europe*. New York: Praeger, 1972.

Sik, Ota. *Plan and Market Under Socialism*. Prague: Academic Publishing House, 1967.

About the Book and Author

In the confrontation between the two main economic systems that has marked the twentieth century, capitalism has been declared the winner—by default—over its adversary, socialism. Today, establishing a market economy has become the primary goal of the formerly socialist countries.

The history of economic reform helps explain this remarkable turning point. Attempts to improve the old centralized system by expanding enterprise autonomy (in Poland, the Soviet Union, and East Germany) and more radical reforms that limited the role of central planning (in Yugoslavia, Czechoslovakia, Hungary, and China) encountered social and political obstacles or had unexpected and undesired effects. During the 1980s, the idea of a socialist market economy, which had been seen as a "third way" between capitalism and centralized socialism, was abandoned as economists gradually came to support a free market rather than the dogma of planning.

Through a comparative and historical analysis of change in socialist and postsocialist systems, this timely and original book clarifies the policies and pitfalls in this extraordinary transition. Bernard Chavance provides a succinct introduction and analysis of the politics and economics of Eastern Europe from the creation of the Stalinist system in the Soviet Union through what he argues have been three major waves of reform since the 1950s to the dismantling of most socialist governments in the 1990s. Exploring the link between the one-party regime and the growing rigidity of socialist economic systems, the author analyzes the failure of both incremental and radical reforms to adapt to new economic challenges, thus leading to the ultimate collapse of communist regimes in Europe.

Bernard Chavance is associate professor at the University of Paris VII. **Charles Hauss** teaches in the Public and International Affairs Department of George Mason University.

Index